The Prompt Engineer

The Little Book Of

A.I. Prompts

Volume One

The Prompt Engineer

P.R.Whitley
Akasha Rehn

RHUBARB
BRIDGE

ISBN: 978-1-9193517-0-4

First Edition, 2025
Published by Rhubarb Bridge Ltd
Created by TechEyeSpy
Printed in British Isles and United States

Rhubarb Bridge • Silicon Fen • British Isles

10 9 8 7 6 5 4 3 2 1

FORWARD

There is a quiet revolution taking place in how we write, reason, and create. Once, words were purely human, improvised fragments of memory and instinct, arranged by intuition.
Today, they are collaborative instruments. The machines have entered the conversation.

The Prompt Trilogy exists to document that change. It is a series not about machines themselves, but about what happens when human language becomes the interface to everything. Across these volumes, we explore how text and thought intertwine: how ideas are distilled into instructions, how creativity adapts to collaboration, and how reasoning evolves when reflected through an artificial mind.

This first volume, The Prompt Engineer, examines the foundation of that practice, the act of designing effective prompts and the discipline required to do it well. The following books will extend that foundation, moving from construction to diffusion, and finally toward reflection: how prompts become tools of authorship, research, and identity.

While the technology is new, the impulse is ancient. Humanity has always sought to shape tools that respond to intention.
What changes now is the speed and subtlety of that dialogue. These books are written for those who want to understand it before the world forgets how recent it all was.

Volume One - The Prompt Engineer
Volume Two - The Prompt Artist
Volume Three - The Prompt Manager

P.R Whitley
TechEyeSpy

INTRODUCTION

Language has always been an act of engineering. Long before algorithms or neural networks existed, every writer, scientist, and diplomat learned that words are mechanisms: they convert thought into form and form into consequence. To prompt a machine, therefore, is not to summon magic but to refine the oldest human skill, the construction of meaning through deliberate structure. The art of prompting begins the moment one stops speaking casually and starts writing as if the sentence itself were a circuit.

The rise of artificial intelligence has not replaced language; it has made language measurable. A computer can now model the probabilities that follow every word, predicting what might come next with astonishing fluency, yet without comprehension. It mimics the surface of thought while lacking its interior. The prompt is therefore both key and compass a design document that instructs the model how to travel across possibility space..

Large Language Model (LLM)
An AI system trained on vast text data to predict the most likely next words in a sequence.

Each time you type a prompt, you are engaging with an immense linguistic engine.

Inside that engine, billions of parameters weigh relationships between words the way synapses might weigh sensations.

It does not reason, but it recognises patterns of reasoning. When you ask for an explanation or a story, it performs a simulation of human coherence an echo that appears intelligent because the statistics of language and the psychology of thought share similar shapes.

Prompt
A written input or instruction that guides a model's output by shaping probability patterns

To work effectively with such a system requires a shift in mindset. You are not commanding intelligence; you are programming probability. Every phrase you use alters the statistical field in which the model predicts. Change a single verb, and the result may veer in tone, detail, or perspective. This volatility is not error; it is the nature of a probabilistic machine.

Many first-time users mistake this variation for inconsistency. They expect the machine to behave deterministically the same input producing the same output because that is how conventional software behaves. But a large language model does not execute code; it generates continuations. It rolls a weighted die billions of times per second, producing language that balances between repetition and novelty. Its strength is not certainty but adaptability.

If you ask the same question twice and receive two different answers, you have not caught the model lying. You have glimpsed the internal turbulence of probability space. A prompt engineer's task is to stabilise that turbulence to phrase questions in ways that anchor meaning without suffocating creativity. This is why prompting resembles both mathematics and poetry. It demands precision and openness in equal measure.

When people say that artificial intelligence sometimes "hallucinates," they describe this same uncertainty from another angle. The model fills gaps in its knowledge by continuing the statistical story rather than consulting a database. It cannot know that it is wrong because it cannot know anything at all. What it produces is a plausible continuation, and plausibility is often mistaken for truth. The role of the engineer is not merely to instruct but to verify.

Probabilistic Generation

The process by which an AI selects its next word according to statistical likelihood rather than understanding.

To engineer a prompt well is to learn to think in the machine's language not its vocabulary, but its structure. That structure is mathematical and linguistic at once, and it rewards clarity above all. Ambiguity, which humans tolerate and often enjoy, is poison to a model. Where a person might find charm in suggestion, a model finds confusion. It interprets a word not as feeling but as coordinate, a point in an immense semantic grid.

Hallucination
Plausible but false text produced when the model fills missing data with statistically likely patterns.

Every misplaced modifier, every unanchored pronoun, widens the field of possible continuations and thereby weakens control. A prompt engineer must learn to compress uncertainty the way an architect controls stress in a beam. The goal is not to write beautifully but to write unambiguously to craft sentences that perform one clear function. This is not creativity's opposite; it is its foundation. Once structure exists, imagination can flow without collapse.

Every misplaced modifier, every unanchored pronoun, widens the field of possible continuations and thereby weakens control. A prompt engineer must learn to compress uncertainty the way an architect controls stress in a beam. The goal is not to write beautifully but to write unambiguousl to craft sentences that perform one clear function. This is not creativity's opposite; it is its foundation. Once structure exists, imagination can flow without collapse.

Prompting, then, is less a technical trick than a new literacy. It requires one to unlearn casual speech and rediscover precision as a creative force. To write for a machine is to rediscover grammar as physics every word a vector, every clause a constraint.

Ambiguit
Linguistic uncertainty that allows multiple valid interpretations of the same text.

Those who master this will not only obtain better answers; they will shape the very grammar of human–machine collaboration. The next pages are written for those who wish to do precisely that.

To work fluently with a language model, one must first accept that language itself behaves like code. The sentence becomes a function; its punctuation, an operator. Human readers tolerate imprecision because context rescues them. Machines, however, do not infer beyond the data provided. The model observes only the sequence of tokens before it fragments of text transformed into numerical vectors that describe position, frequency, and relation. Within that abstraction lies its entire world.

Each token is mapped in a high-dimensional space where meaning is measured not by definition but by proximity. Words that appear together in human writing tend to cluster together in this mathematical universe. "Sun" and "light" occupy nearby coordinates; "sun" and "bureaucracy" are far apart. When you write a prompt, you are tracing a path through that terrain, and the model continues your trajectory based on where the statistical gravity points.

This explains why sentence structure matters more than most users realise. The model is not reading; it is aligning probabilities. Place a key term at the end of a clause and you alter its weight. Repeat a noun and you increase its statistical prominence. A prompt written without awareness of this logic behaves like an equation with missing brackets it may run, but the result is unstable.

Token
The smallest unit of text processed by an AI model, often a full word or part of one, represented as a numeric vector.

The attention system is the heart of every large language model. It calculates which words depend on which others, dynamically re-evaluating context as it writes. Attention gives the illusion of focus; it allows the model to seem aware of relationships within a sentence. Yet it has no memory beyond its window of visibility. Once the text scrolls beyond that limit, earlier words fade from calculation. This technical fact explains the gradual loss of coherence in long exchanges.

Engineers learn to design within these boundaries the way pilots learn to navigate airspace. When a model "forgets," it is not malfunctioning; it has simply reached the end of its computational horizon. The solution is not complaint but architecture. By summarising, recapping, or modularising prompts, the human designer extends continuity artificially. The prompt becomes an engineered bridge between fragments of machine attention.

Attention Mechanism
The process by which a transformer model assigns relative importance to different tokens when generating the next word.vector.

Because every model sees language statistically, syntax functions as control logic. A missing comma can shift probability weight in the same way a misplaced parenthesis breaks a line of code. Punctuation defines relationships between tokens, signalling how the machine should group them in its internal map. When you write a prompt, you are not only instructing a system you are shaping its probability landscape with grammar as your instrument.

Context Window
The maximum number of tokens a model can use at one time to generate a response before older information is dropped.next word.vector.

Precision in this context is not pedantry; it is mechanical necessity. If you wish the model to describe A before B, you must specify that order explicitly. If you want comparison rather than substitution, you must mark that relationship in the phrasing. The prompt engineer's goal is to reduce ambiguity to a point where every next word generated remains aligned with intent, even when the model's creative variability is active.

This predictability emerges only through discipline. Like any engineer, the practitioner tests, observes, and refines. Over time, one learns that good prompts are less about clever wording and more about consistent structure. The magic disappears, replaced by a reliable craft. The surprise is that reliability itself becomes creative a new form of expression born from constraint.

When you begin to think in this way, language transforms into a system of levers. Every conjunction, every modifier, every bracket becomes an instrument of control. The model is not responding to your meaning but to your mathematics to the probabilities that your wording constructs. Precision is how you translate thought into pattern, and pattern into predictable behaviour. This is the essence of engineering with language.

The following chapters will move from this foundation from grammar as structure into the active practice of design: how to build prompts that think in sequences, refine themselves through iteration, and maintain coherence over time. But first, you must understand that prompting is not an act of expression. It is an act of construction. The machine cannot intuit what you intend; it can only calculate what you write. Everything depends on how well you build the sentence.

Syntax
The arrangement of words and punctuation that governs how a language model interprets relationships between tokens.

The first instinct of anyone learning to work with an artificial intelligence is to over-explain. Faced with the unpredictability of machine dialogue, the beginner compensates with detail every instruction specified, every contingency written out. Yet the paradox of prompting is that excessive precision can obscure rather than clarify. The longer the instruction, the more pathways the model must calculate, and the weaker each individual pathway becomes. True clarity arises not from abundance, but from proportion.

Constraint
A defined limit (on words, tone, or structure) used to focus and stabilise a model's output.

A prompt with high instruction density contains little waste. Each word contributes to direction rather than decoration. A low-density prompt, by contrast, confuses the model with redundancy or irrelevance. The goal is not to compress for brevity's sake, but to ensure that every element performs a role in the system. Just as engineers remove excess wiring to reduce signal noise, the prompt engineer removes surplus phrasing to reduce interpretive noise.

Machines do not reward verbosity. They respond to structure. When a prompt becomes a paragraph of stipulations, the model begins to diffuse its attention, allocating probability across too many weak cues. Important details compete with trivial ones. The result is an output that feels blurred technically correct, linguistically fluent, yet somehow hollow. Precision fails not because of what is missing, but because of what was added without necessity.

Instruction Density
The ratio between the number of words in a prompt and the amount of usable information they convey.

Entropy in prompting is easy to recognise: a response that starts correctly, wanders off course, then forgets the task altogether. The cause is not laziness on the model's part but excess freedom within the instruction set. Each unnecessary clause widens the probability space, forcing the system to average between competing meanings. What emerges is neither accurate nor creative merely statistically safe.

The art of clarity, then, lies in controlled omission. You must learn what not to say. The best prompt contains enough information to define boundaries but leaves enough space for inference within those boundaries. This is the difference between clarity and completeness. Completeness is exhaustive; clarity is selective. To pursue the former is to drown the model in text. To master the latter is to give the model just enough scaffolding to climb the idea unaided.

This principle mirrors how human cognition works under instruction. A novice learns faster when the guidance is simple and specific, not encyclopaedic. A good teacher frames the task, demonstrates the pattern, then allows exploration. A prompt should do the same. It defines a vector, not a cage. Each phrase is a nudge toward a direction, not a barrier against alternatives.

Yet the boundary between under- and over-specification is narrow. Too little context, and the model reverts to generic averages. Too much, and it collapses into rigidity. The balance depends on purpose. Analytical tasks demand constraint; creative tasks demand tolerance. The prompt engineer learns to tune this relationship as finely as a musician tunes tension in a string enough resistance to hold form, enough slack to resonate.

Information Entropy

A measure of disorder within a system; in language models, it reflects the uncertainty caused by excessive or conflicting instruction.

The discipline required is not linguistic ornament but conceptual economy. To engineer well is to think hierarchically: which parts of the request are essential, which are optional, and which are decorative? Every prompt can be divided into these layers. The process of iteration, discussed later, is nothing more than refining that hierarchy until efficiency replaces guesswork.

By recognising hierarchy, you teach the machine to reason in the same pattern you do. It begins at the top of the structure, the goal and descends through the supporting details in logical order. Without hierarchy, it drifts laterally, mistaking emphasis for randomness. Order gives the illusion of comprehension. In its absence, even the most powerful model becomes erratic.

Clarity, then, is not simplicity alone; it is balance.
The well-engineered prompt has no spare parts. It achieves completeness not by writing everything, but by writing the right things in the right sequence. The remainder is noise, and noise is entropy a tax on meaning that every engineer learns to pay only once.

Every engineer, at some point, meets the unsettling truth that the same prompt rarely produces the same result twice. The instinct is to blame the system. Perhaps the servers changed, or the model "forgot" something, or a hidden bias interfered. In reality, the variation is fundamental. A large language model is not a database of answers. It is a probability engine, and probability is, by nature, unstable when left unconstrained.

Hierarchy
The ordered structure within a prompt that ranks information by importance, guiding the model's attention.

Each time the model writes a word, it considers thousands of possible continuations, each carrying a likelihood score. The model then samples from that distribution sometimes choosing the most probable word, sometimes one that is merely plausible. This is why responses differ even under identical instructions: each run is a new sequence of probabilistic draws. To the machine, language is a series of weighted dice rolls that collectively approximate coherence.

Reproducibility, therefore, must be engineered. It is not a default property. To make an AI consistent, you must restrict its range of choices. This is achieved through control parameters that shape the sampling process, narrowing the set of acceptable outputs until the machine's behaviour becomes statistically predictable.

At a temperature near zero, the model behaves deterministically. It always selects the most probable next word. The result is consistent but often lifeless, because creativity depends on uncertainty. Raise the temperature, and diversity returns ideas unfold in unexpected ways, but precision weakens. Each project demands its own equilibrium. Technical writing favours stability; brainstorming thrives on turbulence.

Another important variable, often less understood, is top-k or top-p sampling thresholds that limit how many of the most probable tokens the model can consider at each step. By adjusting these values, an engineer sculpts the breadth of imagination within the model. The smaller the threshold, the narrower the thought process; the larger, the more diffuse the reasoning. This is probability design, not magic. Every apparent mood or personality shift in an AI arises from the balance between these numbers.

Temperature

A control setting that adjusts randomness during sampling; low values make results more repetitive, high values increase variation.

Understanding this machinery removes the illusion of capricious intelligence. What users often describe as "mood" or "style" in a model is simply variance under different sampling conditions. An engineer who learns to manipulate these settings can tune the same model to act like a careful analyst one moment and a reckless poet the next. What feels like personality is parameterisation.

Yet even within fixed parameters, small differences persist. Minor updates to the model weights, variations in hardware precision, or stochastic rounding in the numerical layers can all cause divergence. These microscopic perturbations accumulate. Over thousands of token generations, they shift the trajectory of the text. Perfect reproducibility, therefore, is mathematically impossible. The language model's architecture is built on floating-point arithmetic a form of controlled chaos that ensures no path is ever precisely retraced.

Top-k / Top-p Sampling
Methods for limiting how many of the highest-probability tokens are eligible for selection, controlling diversity and focus in output.

For professionals, this limitation is not a flaw but a design constraint. It requires the same attitude that scientists adopt toward measurement error: expect variation, and control it statistically. The prompt engineer learns to measure outcomes by distribution rather than instance. A good prompt is one that yields a reliable range of acceptable answers, not an identical sentence every time. The discipline lies in knowing how much variation is tolerable for the task.

Floating-Point Precision
The numerical format used in computation; tiny rounding variations can alter outcomes across repeated runs.

When consistency truly matters as in automation, policy writing, or scientific documentation reproducibility must be imposed from outside. Scripts can fix parameters, lock random seeds, or route prompts through controlled templates. In these cases, prompting becomes software engineering, not conversation. But when exploration is the goal, the variability of the model becomes an ally. It allows discovery through difference, producing insights that no fixed system could invent.

In this sense, unpredictability is not a weakness of artificial intelligence; it is its animating principle. It mirrors the variability of human thought not by design, but by coincidence of mathematics. The engineer's challenge is to convert that noise into useful texture. By learning how randomness functions, you learn how creativity survives within computation.

This is the paradox of the unrepeatable machine: it never says the same thing twice, yet it always speaks from the same foundation. The structure is stable; the expression, infinite. To work with such a system is to accept that control is partial, precision conditional, and consistency a negotiated outcome. Prompt engineering, at its highest level, is the discipline of mastering uncertainty.

Every prompt begins as language, but not every piece of language qualifies as a prompt. The difference is intention. Ordinary writing aims to persuade, express, or entertain; prompt writing aims to construct alignment between a human concept and a machine's statistical space. The prompt engineer does not merely communicate with a model but calibrates it, ensuring that the meanings inside the human mind map correctly onto the representations inside the machine.

Framing
The contextual boundary that defines how a model should interpret a request or concept.

In practice, semantic alignment is an act of translation. The human world runs on context, emotion, and assumption; the model's world runs on patterns, probabilities, and associations. Between those worlds lies a gulf of interpretation that only structure can bridge. The prompt functions as that bridge. Each clause must convert ambiguity into architecture. When alignment is achieved, the model's probabilities converge on the same conceptual centre the human occupies, and communication becomes collaboration.

The professional learns quickly that words behave differently in this environment. In conversation, language is elastic; we rely on tone, gesture, and shared history to fill gaps. The model, by contrast, possesses none of these cues. It interprets "write a summary" not as an instruction imbued with human pragmatism but as a literal pattern to reproduce. Without explicit framing, it cannot know whether brevity, accuracy, or elegance is your priority. The engineer's role is to supply that hierarchy of meaning in advance.

This is why prompting cannot remain intuitive. It must become procedural. Each sentence you write becomes part of a controlled system designed to minimise misalignment. You learn to anticipate failure modes the way an electrical engineer anticipates resistance. If a circuit sparks, the design is at fault. If a model drifts, the prompt is at fault. Through iteration and testing, prompting matures from conversation into specification the blueprint of an intended outcome.

Semantic Alignment
The degree to which a model's generated meaning matches the user's intended meaning.

Prompt Engineer

Language, once treated as art, now functions as infrastructure. It carries not feeling but force. To design effectively is to understand that words have measurable behaviour inside an LLM. They exert pressure on probability flows; they redirect the model's internal attention. When you master this behaviour, you move from speaking to the machine to designing through it. The prompt becomes a system interface, a language of control and collaboration.

As professional practice evolves, this shift in thinking defines a new discipline one that fuses linguistics, design, and computation. The prompt engineer becomes neither programmer nor writer but something in between: a translator of intent into statistical geometry. Mastery of this craft demands respect for both sides of the dialogue the human capacity for meaning and the machine's capacity for structure.

The reward for this discipline is consistency. When alignment succeeds, an AI ceases to feel alien. It becomes an instrument that extends human reasoning, not imitates it.
The engineer writes prompts that behave like reliable tools reproducible enough for work, flexible enough for creativity. Each sentence becomes a calibrated vector pointing from question to answer.

This book, and the trilogy that follows, are dedicated to that calibration. The pages ahead treat prompting not as novelty but as professional practice a discipline of design whose materials happen to be words. You will learn to build clarity as if constructing architecture, to test language as if debugging software, and to think of communication as a system of forces.

By the end of this first volume, you will understand prompting not as dialogue but as engineering the deliberate shaping of meaning so that a machine can traverse it without error. The following chapter begins where all engineering begins: with structure, clarity, and the physics of language.

CONTENTS

PROFILE:

ELON MUSK

CEO, Tesla / Founder, xAI

Elon Musk is a South African-born American entrepreneur, inventor, and engineer whose ventures have shaped the modern technology landscape across industries ranging from space exploration to electric vehicles and artificial intelligence. He is best known as the CEO of Tesla, the aerospace company SpaceX, and most recently, as the founder of xAI, a company focused on developing safe and transparent artificial intelligence.

Musk was also an early backer and co-founder of OpenAI, the organization behind ChatGPT, before stepping away from its board in 2018. With degrees in physics and economics from the University of Pennsylvania, Musk has long emphasized the existential risks associated with unregulated AI development, warning of its potential to surpass human control.

"With artificial intelligence we are summoning the demon."

Chapter 1
The Architecture of Clarity

Prompts as Code: Syntax, Tokens, and Implicit Grammar

Every effective prompt begins as a piece of language, but it behaves like a line of code. The words you choose compile into mathematics. Each noun, verb, or connector becomes a token a discrete instruction that the model interprets as numerical coordinates in a vast semantic space. When those coordinates line up correctly, the system flows smoothly from one idea to the next. When they collide or contradict, the result is linguistic noise that looks like confusion.

To most users, a prompt is a sentence. To a language model, it is a series of vectors projected through thousands of dimensions. The model does not "read" in the human sense; it measures distances between these vectors, mapping how closely one word relates to another. The act of writing a prompt therefore resembles designing an electrical circuit: words are components, syntax is wiring, and meaning is current. Misplace a connector and the current arcs into empty space.

Token
The smallest unit of text a model processes, often a whole word or part of one, represented as a numeric vector.

Human language evolved to be forgiving. We can reorder phrases, break grammar, or imply meaning through tone, and still be understood. Machines have no such tolerance. They interpret linear order as logic, not melody. A misplaced comma can alter which tokens interact; an undefined subject can erase context entirely. For this reason, the prompt engineer must learn to think structurally, to see sentences not as expressions of feeling but as frameworks of control.

Transformer
The neural network architecture that processes all words in a sequence simultaneously to calculate their relationships.

Inside the model, syntax governs probability flow. Each punctuation mark signals how attention should travel between tokens. The transformer architecture that underpins modern models evaluates all relationships at once, assigning weight to each connection. A full stop ends a thought not because the machine recognises grammar, but because the token "." historically correlates with sentence boundaries in its training data. The model continues patterns, not meanings.

Understanding this architecture turns prompting from intuition into engineering. The writer begins to place information with intent, separating context from instruction, description from constraint. Prompts become modular: an initial setup defines identity or scenario, a secondary section lists tasks, and a final clause establishes output conditions. Each part has a structural purpose. When this hierarchy is consistent, the model's reasoning stabilises. It knows which segment frames context and which defines action.

At the lowest level, the model predicts one token at a time. At the highest level, it simulates reasoning by chaining predictions together. Your syntax becomes the skeleton of that reasoning. When clarity falters when clauses overlap or modifiers dangle the probabilities that hold meaning together begin to split. The system fills the gaps with generic continuations because statistics prefer the average to the uncertain. This is how vagueness manifests as cliché.

To engineer clarity is to design these relationships consciously. A well-structured prompt controls how the model allocates its internal focus.
It begins with an anchor the explicit statement of role or goal followed by clear sequencing of tasks.

Hierarchy
The ordered structure within a prompt that ranks information by importance and guides the model's attention.

It ends with boundary tokens that signal closure. Every section exists for a reason. The goal is not to write beautifully but predictably, to make language behave as a deterministic mechanism within a probabilistic machine.

Viewed this way, prompting becomes a grammar of engineering rather than expression. Each time you adjust syntax, you adjust current flow through the network of meaning. A misplaced word is not a stylistic flaw but a circuit error. The clarity you achieve is measurable in behaviour: reduced hallucination, stable tone, consistent formatting. When you begin to think of your sentences as systems, you cease guessing what the model will do you start designing what it can do.

Determinism
A condition in which identical inputs produce identical outputs; in LLMs this occurs only when randomness is restricted.

How A.I. Interprets Context Windows and Weight

Imagine placing a page of text beneath a magnifying lens that can only display a few paragraphs at a time. Everything within that circle is visible, everything outside it forgotten. This is how a large language model perceives information.
It does not store memory from one turn to the next; it only processes the portion of text contained within its active field of view, known as the context window.

Each token inside this window exists as part of a probability network. The model calculates how strongly each token relates to every other, forming a matrix of attention scores. These relationships are recalculated each time new text is added. The older the word in relation to the window boundary, the weaker its influence becomes. When the window overflows, earlier tokens vanish, and with them, the contextual scaffolding that held the conversation steady.

Context Window
The maximum number of tokens a model can process at once before older tokens are discarded.

The effect is subtle but critical. The model never truly forgets an idea it loses access to it. The parameters that govern its behaviour remain unchanged, yet the local relationships that connect one sentence to another dissolve. This is why long conversations drift off-topic, why stories lose their thread, and why prompts that rely on earlier context begin to repeat themselves. The system's world is bounded by its visible text.

For the engineer, this limitation is not an inconvenience but a design parameter. It forces precision in how information is introduced and repeated. If an idea must persist, it must be reintroduced.

If consistency matters, summaries or recaps must be embedded at intervals. The prompt becomes an architecture for memory, a structure that compensates for the absence of memory itself.

Attention Mechanism
The algorithm within a transformer that determines which tokens influence each other most strongly during generation.

Within the window, not all tokens are equal. The model's attention mechanism assigns weight to each one, elevating some and diminishing others based on statistical importance. Words at the start of a sentence tend to exert more influence than those buried in the middle. Proper nouns carry heavier semantic gravity than conjunctions. Repetition amplifies weight; obscurity diffuses it. By understanding this hierarchy, the engineer can deliberately position key information where attention is highest.

Weight can be manipulated through structure. Short, direct sentences strengthen signal; long, meandering clauses dilute it. Bullet points or numbered lists, when the model is capable of interpreting them segment meaning cleanly, reducing ambiguity about scope. Conversely, complex nested instructions compete for attention, often causing partial compliance where the model fulfils one condition but ignores another. Every sentence you write is a negotiation with attention.

Weight can be manipulated through structure.
Short, direct sentences strengthen signal; long, meandering clauses dilute it. Bullet points or numbered lists when the model is capable of interpreting them segment meaning cleanly, reducing ambiguity about scope.

Token Weight
A relative measure of importance assigned to each token by the model's attention layers.

Conversely, complex nested instructions compete for attention, often causing partial compliance where the model fulfils one condition but ignores another. Every sentence you write is a negotiation with attention.

The concept of weight also explains why certain stylistic tricks work inconsistently. Emphasis through capitalisation, brackets, or bold text rarely translates into greater focus unless the model was trained to interpret those patterns. Its perception of importance emerges from probability, not typography. The only reliable form of emphasis is repetition or explicit instruction. If you want the model to remember a constraint, restate it plainly and place it near the end of the prompt, where recency bias amplifies its weight.

Understanding recency allows the engineer to choreograph sequence. The order in which information appears affects the order in which it is processed. Place definitions first and tasks second, and the model interprets subsequent instructions through those definitions. Reverse them, and it improvises meaning. Prompting therefore becomes an act of layout design within language deciding what appears where, and for how long.

Recency Bias
The tendency of a model to prioritise information that appears near the end of the current context window.

When structure is designed with awareness of context and weight, coherence stabilises. The model's attention no longer diffuses across irrelevant fragments; it concentrates where the engineer directs it. In essence, clarity is not merely linguistic it is spatial. The prompt defines the geometry of thought inside a machine that cannot think. Once you learn to design within that geometry, you begin to write not just sentences, but systems.

Constraint
A fixed parameter that limits how a model interprets or formats its output, improving reliability.

Breaking Down Human Sentences into Machine-Readable Intent

A sentence written for a person and a sentence written for a model may look identical, but they do not function the same way. Humans rely on shared experience, social convention, and intuition to fill in meaning; machines rely on structure. To a large language model, there is no context beyond the words it receives. It does not assume, infer, or imagine outside that boundary. Every instruction must be fully self-contained.

When you write, "Explain the significance of Newton's laws for modern engineering," a human teacher knows to summarise history, describe applications, and conclude with commentary. The model, however, recognises only that each of those ideas might be relevant. Without a defined hierarchy or task segmentation, it guesses how much emphasis to give each. Sometimes it begins with physics, sometimes with biography, sometimes with speculation. The output changes because the intent was distributed rather than defined.

Intent Parsing
The process of identifying and isolating the functional goal of a human instruction so that a model can interpret it unambiguously.

A professional prompt therefore begins by separating the sentence into units of intent. What is the core task? What are the supporting requirements? What are optional details? Each of these should become its own clause or instruction. A single prompt might look conversational, but internally it should function like a sequence of logic gates each part triggering a precise operation in order.

Logic Gate (Analogy)
A conceptual model for prompt design, where each clause functions as a conditional trigger determining subsequent behaviour.

Consider how small adjustments change interpretation:

Human phrasing: "Write a short article about renewable energy that sounds optimistic."
Machine-readable phrasing: "Write a 200-word article describing renewable energy technologies. Use positive and forward-looking language."

The meaning is the same, but the structure differs. The rewritten version breaks the original into discrete intents: output length, subject matter, and tone. Each element becomes a measurable constraint. The model no longer has to infer what "short" or "optimistic" means; it has defined parameters to follow.

Breaking sentences in this way also reveals implicit assumptions. Many prompts contain hidden requests the writer never articulates be accurate, stay formal, keep formatting clean. The model cannot guess these unless they are stated. When an engineer audits a prompt, the question to ask is not "What am I saying?" but "What is the model hearing?" The two are rarely identical.

Pseudocode
A simplified, language-agnostic description of logic used to clarify intent without the syntax of a programming language.

A useful exercise is to treat every instruction as a line of pseudocode. For example:

```
TASK: Summarise document
CONSTRAINT: 100 words maximum
TONE: Objective
OUTPUT: Paragraph format
```

This structure clarifies the difference between human style and machine logic. The prompt still reads naturally, but each sentence performs a specific function. The model receives not a vague suggestion but a set of conditions under which probability can stabilise.

The goal is not to strip away humanity from language, but to make intention legible to a system that lacks intuition. Once a prompt is divided into its operative components, you can reassemble it into smooth prose. A model will follow that restructured version far more consistently because its internal parsing aligns with your external logic.

Ambiguity, in this sense, is often just collapsed structure. By expanding a tangled sentence into its underlying instructions, you restore control. The output becomes reproducible not because the machine has improved, but because your language has become measurable.

When you learn to write for the model's logic rather than your own expectation, prompting ceases to feel mysterious. It becomes an act of translation between two forms of intelligence: one organic, one statistical. The engineer's role is not to teach the machine to understand, but to phrase ideas so clearly that understanding becomes unnecessary.

The Anatomy of a Clean Prompt: Scaffolding and Hierarchy

A well-written prompt is not simply clear; it is built. Every element has a function, every function has a position, and every position has a relationship to the others. The design principle behind all effective prompting is hierarchy a layered arrangement of information that tells the model what matters most. Without it, the machine interprets text as a flat sequence of equal importance, drifting between fragments without priority.

The human mind applies hierarchy instinctively. When reading a set of instructions, we know to prioritise main objectives over side notes. A language model lacks this instinct.

Hierarchy
An ordered structure within a prompt that ranks information by importance and guides the model's attention.

It calculates associations, not authority. If every clause appears equal, the model distributes attention equally, often diluting focus across multiple goals. A clean prompt therefore begins by establishing a framework that defines what comes first, what depends on it, and what can vary.

Think of this structure as scaffolding. It holds the task in place while the model builds upon it. Each part of the prompt connects to a specific layer of reasoning: context, role, task, constraints, and output format. These layers act as invisible markers that organise logic inside the model's attention field. When written consistently, they produce results that are both more coherent and easier to debug.

Scaffolding
The layered design of a prompt that separates context, instruction, and constraints to maintain structural clarity.

A professional prompt might appear conversational, yet beneath that tone lies deliberate architecture. The first layer sets context: the background, scenario, or perspective that defines how the model should interpret the task. The second establishes role: who or what the model is meant to simulate analyst, teacher, editor, or designer. The third defines the task itself the main action to perform. The fourth introduces constraints limits of scope, tone, or length. The fifth describes output format the expected structure or medium of the answer. Together these form the skeleton of comprehension.

When these layers are ordered correctly, the model builds its internal logic accordingly. Context activates relevant patterns from training data, role sets the tone, task drives generation, constraints filter possibilities, and output format determines presentation. If the order is reversed for instance, if formatting is described before the model knows what to write the result often becomes inconsistent or incomplete. The model attempts to satisfy structure before content.

Hierarchy also clarifies iteration. Because each layer performs a separate function, you can modify one without destabilising the rest. If the tone feels wrong, adjust the role. If the answer is too long, tighten the constraint. If the model misses context, expand the background. Prompt debugging thus becomes modular a process of tuning layers rather than rewriting the entire instruction.

The clarity gained through scaffolding is both linguistic and cognitive. It forces the writer to externalise intention to ask, What exactly am I asking for, and what do I want it to look like? This act of structuring thought often reveals gaps in reasoning that would otherwise surface as model errors. When you cannot describe your own layers, the prompt will fail before it is tested.

Modularity

The design principle that allows independent adjustment of distinct prompt components without affecting the whole system.

A simple example illustrates the transformation:

Unstructured prompt:
"Write about the challenges of urban farming."

Structured prompt:
Context: "Urban farming combines agriculture with limited city space."
Role: "You are an agricultural analyst writing for policymakers."
Task: "Explain the main challenges urban farms face."
Constraints: "Keep the tone formal and limit to 300 words."
Output Format: "Produce three short paragraphs with clear topic sentences."

The difference is architectural. The second version tells the model not just what to do but how to interpret the act of doing. It divides reasoning into stages and gives each stage boundaries. When executed, the model follows a predictable route: define context, analyse, constrain, and present. The result reads like deliberate authorship rather than statistical improvisation.

Scaffolding also serves a secondary function: it enables scale. When teams collaborate or automate workflows, consistent prompt architecture becomes a shared language. Prompts can be catalogued, versioned, and reused across projects. Each component can be documented and updated independently. In that sense, prompt engineering matures into systems design not one clever phrase at a time, but a repeatable framework of linguistic precision.

Predictability
The consistency of model output achieved when prompt structure limits variation without removing flexibility.

To construct a clean prompt, then, is to respect hierarchy as both a logic and a discipline. The engineer learns to think spatially within language, to design every instruction so that meaning flows downward from context to detail. Once this scaffold is established, the model behaves with stability; it knows what to attend to, and in what order.

In the end, clarity is less about eloquence than architecture.

The sentence is no longer a vehicle for expression; it is a framework for reasoning.

The Hidden Logic of "And," "Or," "Then," and "If"

In human conversation, small connector words often pass unnoticed. They guide rhythm, not logic. Yet to a large language model, connectors are the hidden circuitry of thought. They decide whether the system interprets two ideas as simultaneous, alternative, or conditional. Each carries mathematical consequence: it alters how attention links one part of a sentence to another, redirecting probability like a switch in an electrical circuit.

When you write, "List the pros and cons of solar energy," the word and creates a parallel instruction.
The model must generate two complementary outputs within the same scope one positive, one negative.
If you instead write, "List the pros or cons of solar energy," the connector implies choice, not combination. Most models resolve such prompts by defaulting to balance, providing both lists anyway, because probability favours symmetry. This subtle shift shows how logical precision determines behavioural precision.

The operator then introduces sequence. It signals order, directing the model to complete one step before another.

For example:
"Summarise this article, then suggest three follow-up research questions."

The inclusion of then separates tasks temporally within a single prompt. Without it, the model might blend the summary and the questions together, losing distinction between analysis and generation. Because a model predicts linearly, sequence must be made explicit. It cannot infer process from context alone.

Logical Operators
Words such as and, or, then, and if that control how a model links or separates reasoning steps within a prompt.

The most complex of the connectors, if, introduces conditional logic. Conditionals do not exist naturally in human prose; they belong to computation. Yet the model treats them as branching instructions, generating alternate continuations depending on how the clause resolves statistically.

Parallel Instruction
Aa prompt structure that asks the model to handle multiple subtasks simultaneously rather than sequentially.

For instance:
"If the text is longer than 300 words, shorten it; otherwise, keep it unchanged."

Here, the word if creates a simulated branch in reasoning.
The model evaluates the condition implicitly by analysing its own text, then follows the corresponding clause.
In more advanced prompting frameworks, explicit conditionals are implemented programmatically, but even in plain language, if guides probability flow as a form of linguistic logic gate.

The engineer must also consider the compound effects of connectors. Chains like "and then" or "if... then... and finally" can overload a model's reasoning if written without hierarchy.
Each operator opens or closes a new logical path, consuming tokens as it maintains internal coherence. Excessive nesting increases entropy, creating competing probabilities that degrade precision.
It is often better to separate such instructions into multiple prompts or structured lists than to embed them all within one long sentence.

Sequential Prompting
A design pattern where tasks are performed in a defined order to maintain logical progression.

This is why conjunctions and conditionals are the engineer's most delicate tools. They govern not what the model knows but how it moves through what it knows. Each operator is a lever that defines relationship: and unites, or divides, then sequences, if branches.
By mastering these levers, you learn to choreograph reasoning rather than merely request it.

Prompting, when reduced to essentials, is the control of logic through language. In a system that has no inherent understanding, connection words become the machinery of meaning.
They are not decoration but design the syntax that converts text into structured thought.

Conditional Prompting
Instructing the model to alter its behaviour depending on a stated condition or contextual trigger.

Testing for Ambiguity: The Echo Test

Once a prompt is written, it should not be trusted. Even the clearest instruction can conceal ambiguity invisible to its author. The engineer's task is to reveal that ambiguity before it causes error. Unlike traditional software, prompting has no compiler to catch misalignment.
There is only language and probability. The best way to test a prompt is to let the model expose its own misunderstanding a technique known as the echo test.

The echo test is deceptively simple: you ask the model to summarise your instruction before carrying it out.

For example:
"Before responding, summarise what you believe this prompt is asking you to do."

The model's paraphrase reveals its internal interpretation not the literal syntax, but the pattern of priorities it detected. Any difference between your intention and its echo is a map of ambiguity. Where your focus was on precision, its summary may emphasise creativity; where you expected analysis, it may assume opinion. Each drift is diagnostic.

> Echo Test
> A diagnostic method in which a model restates a prompt in its own words to reveal differences between intended and interpreted meaning.

This process is valuable because ambiguity often hides in grammar, not content. A clause placed too early or too late can shift the model's weight of attention. The echo exposes such imbalances by showing which sections dominate the model's understanding.

> Prompt Ambiguity
> A condition in which multiple valid interpretations of an instruction exist, causing unpredictable or inconsistent output.

If a minor note appears in the echo but the main task does not, hierarchy has failed. Adjust the structure, re-test, and compare again until the model's summary mirrors your intent without deviation.

The echo test also serves a secondary purpose: it quantifies misunderstanding. By measuring how many revisions are required before interpretation stabilises, an engineer can estimate a prompt's clarity score informally. Prompts that align on the first or second attempt are strong; those requiring multiple rephrasings contain unresolved ambiguity. This iterative verification process transforms prompting from intuition into engineering practice.

Some professionals use variants of the echo test to verify role fidelity.

For instance:
"Summarise your assigned role and objectives before completing the task."

This confirms that the model has retained the correct perspective scientist, journalist, tutor before generating the final answer. If the echo misidentifies its role, the preceding instruction chain has failed to anchor context.

A second variant checks constraint compliance:
"Restate the limits and conditions you are expected to follow."

This reveals whether length, tone, or style restrictions have been understood. Inconsistent compliance is rarely due to disobedience; it reflects poor constraint visibility inside the prompt hierarchy.

Each test not only verifies understanding but teaches you where structure must be reinforced.

Role Fidelity
The model's ability to maintain the identity, tone, or perspective assigned to it throughout generation.

Echo testing closes the loop between design and outcome. It transforms the model from a passive respondent into an analytical partner. By auditing its interpretation, you audit your own clarity. When the echo becomes indistinguishable from intent, the prompt can be considered structurally sound.

At that point, variation in results will stem not from confusion but from controlled randomness a tolerable form of entropy that belongs to creative probability, not linguistic error.

The professional habit of testing every prompt in this way separates engineering from guesswork. Each cycle of refinement reduces interpretive noise until the language behaves predictably.

Over time, the engineer builds an internal sense for ambiguity a sensitivity to phrasing that anticipates where misunderstanding will arise. Echo testing becomes less a procedure than a reflex, integrated into the act of writing itself.

The model, in this sense, becomes its own validator. It cannot understand meaning, but it can mirror it accurately enough to show when alignment fails. Through that reflection, the engineer achieves what software compilers have provided for decades: a system of feedback. Prompting, once iterative and uncertain, becomes measurable, inspectable, and reproducible.

When this discipline is mastered, clarity is no longer an abstract virtue. It becomes a mechanical property of language a design parameter that can be tuned, tested, and confirmed. The next chapter begins from this point of stability, where structure is no longer the problem, and attention turns instead to precision: how small linguistic changes produce large shifts in reasoning.

Controlled Randomness variability that occurs within defined and acceptable limits, maintaining fidelity to the user's intent.

Chapter 2
Precision and Iteration

The Iterative Loop: How Every Failed Response Teaches the System

A prompt is never finished on the first attempt. In engineering, no design survives its prototype, and language is no exception. The difference between a casual user and a professional prompt engineer is not eloquence but patience the willingness to refine, measure, and repeat until variation becomes understanding. Each iteration transforms uncertainty into information. The model does not learn from these revisions, but you do.

When an AI gives a flawed or incomplete answer, that output is not a failure; it is data. The text reveals how the system interpreted your words what it emphasised, ignored, or misread.
Each unwanted paragraph, every missing detail, is a diagnostic signal pointing to ambiguity in the original prompt. The goal is not to fix the model, but to fix the language that produced the misunderstanding.

This feedback loop mirrors scientific experimentation. You begin with a hypothesis a prompt designed to elicit a specific response. You run the experiment and observe the results. You then adjust the variables, re-test, and record the difference. Over time, patterns emerge. The engineer learns not what the model knows, but how it behaves under linguistic stress.

Precision develops through comparison. By analysing differences between successive iterations, you begin to see how subtle changes in phrasing alter probability flow. A word added for politeness might dilute instruction strength; a reordering of clauses might shift the model's focus from reasoning to style.
Through repetition, you discover linguistic leverage the smallest edits that produce the greatest stability.

Iteration
The process of repeatedly refining a prompt through feedback and observation to improve clarity, accuracy, or tone.

Feedback Loop
A cyclic process in which a model's output is analysed and used to modify the input for improved performance.

To record this process is essential. Iteration without documentation becomes superstition. Every professional maintains a prompt log, noting not only results but the reasoning behind each adjustment. The record of what failed is often more valuable than the list of what worked. Failures define the model's boundaries the edges where probability collapses and new methods must be devised.

The most effective way to iterate is incrementally. Alter one element at a time: length, order, or specificity. Changing several factors at once conceals cause and effect. This controlled refinement mirrors the engineering principle of isolating variables.
The practice trains perception; you begin to feel the mechanics of language interacting with the model's statistical geometry.

When you modify only one parameter and observe the output shift predictably, you are witnessing the alignment between structure and behaviour the confirmation that the system is behaving as designed. That moment is the essence of precision.

Iteration also develops intuition about diminishing returns. Early revisions produce dramatic improvements; later ones yield refinement measured in nuance. Knowing when to stop is itself a form of engineering judgement.

The perfect prompt does not exist; only prompts that are optimal for their purpose. Beyond that point, each additional edit adds complexity faster than it adds control. Precision becomes overfitting.

Prompt Log
A written record of prompt versions, parameters, and results, maintained to track refinement and reproducibility.

The discipline of iteration separates professional practice from mere curiosity. It turns prompting into an empirical process one that values documentation, patience, and reproducibility. Each cycle through the loop reduces entropy, transforming randomness into structure and intuition into design. Through this, the prompt engineer becomes not a writer chasing inspiration, but a designer constructing reliability.

The next section will examine the complementary process to iteration:
How precision itself can be used to remove distortion from the model's responses the art of de-biasing through progressive specificity.

De-biasing Through Progressive Specificity

Every model carries the fingerprint of its training data. It has read vast portions of the internet the arguments, preferences, and prejudices of millions of people. From this, it learns patterns of language, not principles of fairness. When asked to describe a profession, it repeats statistical tendencies; when asked to write a story, it inherits cultural defaults. This embedded inclination toward certain perspectives is what we call bias.

Bias does not mean the system has opinions. It means that some words, contexts, and associations occur more often in its training material than others. The model reproduces these imbalances mechanically, unaware that they exist.

A prompt such as "Describe a successful entrepreneur" might, by default, produce a male name and Western background, because those features dominate the historical text it has read. To correct this behaviour, one must intervene linguistically.

Bias
A statistical tendency in model output that reflects the frequency or framing of patterns within its training data.

The first step in de-biasing is awareness. You must assume bias is always present and detectable through testing. Run the same prompt several times with minor changes in phrasing, or vary demographic variables while keeping the task constant. Patterns will appear. Certain answers cluster more tightly than others, revealing where probability density favours one outcome. These are not flaws to condemn but patterns to manage. They tell you how the model's internal map of the world is shaped.

Probability Density
A concentration of likelihood values within a model's statistical space where certain associations dominate others.

De-biasing begins with progressive specificity adding precision step by step until ambiguity is reduced without over-constraint. The process starts by identifying where generality invites assumption.

For instance:

General prompt: "Write about a doctor who changed lives."
Specific prompt: "Write about a doctor, of any gender or background, who improved patient outcomes through innovation."

The second version neutralises demographic defaults by defining scope explicitly. It removes cultural and gender bias without prescribing a single identity. Each clause functions as a linguistic boundary, guiding the model toward balanced probability zones.

Progressive specificity can also correct tone and perspective bias. Suppose a model consistently writes about environmental policy in optimistic terms. By adding modifiers such as "Provide both positive and negative economic consequences," you rebalance sentiment distribution. The technique does not erase bias; it redistributes probability so that neglected perspectives gain representation.

Another layer of de-biasing involves counter-examples. If a model continually outputs stereotypical imagery for example, associating "nurse" with "female" you can explicitly state a neutral or contrasting example within the prompt. The model, recognising that such associations are now less certain, recalculates its probabilities and produces more balanced results. This method works because LLMs prioritise recency and frequency within the context window. Adding neutralising examples shifts their short-term attention away from historical bias.

However, excessive specificity introduces new distortions. When prompts become too prescriptive, they cease to describe probability and begin to enforce ideology. The engineer's goal is balance, not censorship. The test of success is consistency: if neutral phrasing produces a distribution of answers across diverse cases without forced equality, the language is functioning as intended. True de-biasing is probabilistic, not moral.

Professional practice therefore depends on controlled testing. Each modification to a prompt must be compared against a baseline.
When differences in tone, representation, or framing diminish across multiple runs, the engineer records the refined version as a more stable configuration. The model has not changed, but the linguistic interface has been tuned to resist inherited imbalance.

Over time, this process cultivates a discipline of neutrality. The engineer learns to write in ways that reduce assumption without diluting meaning a precision of thought expressed through linguistic restraint. In this sense, de-biasing is not only an ethical task but an aesthetic one. It produces cleaner, more deliberate prompts that describe the world as possibility rather than prejudice.

Bias cannot be removed from data, but it can be counterweighted by design. Through progressive specificity, the engineer restores equilibrium between representation and intention. What emerges is not an unbiased machine such a thing cannot exist but a stable interface through which the human can guide probability toward fairness, one word at a time.

Recency Weighting
The model's tendency to assign higher importance to information that appears later in the prompt or conversation.

Controlling for Tone Drift and Conceptual Slippage

Every conversation with a model is an act of balance. At the start, tone and focus align perfectly; the system responds within the frame you designed. But as the exchange grows longer, entropy begins to accumulate. The model drifts not out of defiance, but out of probability. Words at the top of the context window lose influence. The centre of gravity shifts from your original intention to whatever pattern is most statistically consistent with the recent dialogue. This phenomenon is called tone drift.

Tone drift emerges because large language models do not preserve "state" the way software programs do. They regenerate reasoning at each new step based on visible text only. If that visible text contains emotional cues, subtle sarcasm, or stylistic inconsistency, the system adapts to them immediately. It imitates the latest pattern rather than the initial instruction. What feels like forgetfulness is actually hyper-attention to the most recent data.

Tone Drift
The gradual change in voice, style, or formality that occurs as a model's attention reweights toward newer context.

The related phenomenon, conceptual slippage, arises when the topic itself begins to migrate. A discussion about urban planning may slowly transform into an essay on architecture; a technical breakdown of sensors may start speculating about ethics.

The model's predictive core seeks coherence above accuracy it follows linguistic pathways that appear natural to its training rather than logical to your goal. Without reinforcement, the probability field gradually bends toward generic associations.

Context Reweighting
The process by which a model continually recalculates which tokens are most relevant within its current window of attention.

To counter both drift and slippage, professional practice relies on contextual anchoring the deliberate reintroduction of key phrases, tone markers, or framing sentences at regular intervals. These anchors function as refresh points, restoring the model's awareness of original intent before entropy accumulates beyond recovery.

For example:

"Continue analysing in the same formal academic tone as above."
"Before answering, restate the central question briefly to ensure focus."

Each of these statements re-establishes probability weight on the intended style and topic. The model then realigns its output accordingly. Anchors are linguistic checkpoints that recalibrate the system without requiring full repetition of the prompt.

Another method involves embedding tone descriptors within the structural layers of the prompt itself. Instead of telling the model to "sound professional" in passing, make tone a permanent constraint inside the scaffolding.

Example:

Role: "You are a financial analyst writing for institutional investors."
Constraint: "Maintain a neutral, data-driven tone throughout."

Because tone is now a structural element rather than a surface cue, it persists longer. The model recognises it as part of the logical frame, not as temporary context.

Contextual Anchor
A recurring phrase or instruction used to stabilise tone, structure, or focus within an ongoing model interaction.

For extended conversations or long-form writing, engineers sometimes use recap prompts short summaries that restate accumulated context in condensed form. These recaps act like checkpoints, replacing degraded memory with a fresh, concise version of the original direction.

Example:

"In summary, this discussion focuses on satellite imaging for crop analysis. The goal remains technical accuracy and consistent academic tone."

The recap condenses thousands of earlier tokens into a few sentences that re-anchor the conversation's trajectory. It keeps the model operating inside a defined corridor of meaning.

Professional prompt engineering treats drift not as error but as entropy management. Every system tends toward disorder unless energy is reapplied in this case, linguistic energy. The reassertion of structure, tone, and purpose acts as the energy that restores order. Without it, the conversation naturally decays into statistical inertia, repeating common phrases and losing conceptual tension.

By designing prompts that anticipate drift, you replace correction with prevention. You build redundancy into your language anchors, tone descriptors, recaps so that the model continually reorients itself.

The result is sustained coherence across thousands of words, a quality essential to technical writing, documentation, and long analytical tasks.

Recap Prompt
A short restatement of key context inserted periodically to refresh focus and preserve continuity across long outputs.

When managed correctly, this process yields stability without rigidity. The model remains responsive but not erratic, consistent but not mechanical. Its voice holds steady while its reasoning remains flexible. Precision here is not about constraint alone; it is about controlled adaptability the art of guiding change without letting it unravel purpose.

The next section will examine the mathematical aspect of refinement why brevity amplifies clarity, and how The Mathematics of Revision demonstrates that shorter, denser prompts often outperform verbose ones in both reliability and reasoning quality.

The Mathematics of Revision: Why Shorter Is Often Smarter

Language models operate on numbers, not nuance. Every word is a data point; every sentence, an equation. When a prompt grows too long, the model must distribute its attention across a widening field of tokens. Each token dilutes the influence of the others, and coherence begins to fade. The mathematics of clarity is simple: as word count increases, signal-to-noise ratio decreases. In prompting, verbosity is not depth it is drag.

The effect is measurable. Inside the model's attention mechanism, each token competes for weight. The total attention budget is finite; doubling the text does not double understanding. Instead, it halves focus per unit of meaning. This creates an attention economy within the prompt a trade-off between richness and resolution. The more tokens you spend describing the task, the less sharply each individual instruction is perceived.

Professional prompt engineers learn to write with mathematical precision, reducing words until each carries quantifiable purpose. The goal is not minimalism for aesthetic reasons but for statistical efficiency. A shorter, cleaner prompt allows the model to form stronger internal connections between critical tokens, producing responses that are both faster and more stable. The fewer paths the system must evaluate, the less opportunity for drift or error. The process of revision therefore follows an equation:

> Attention Budget
> The limited computational capacity a model distributes among tokens when determining relevance and relationships.

$$\text{Clarity} = \text{Information} \div \text{Tokens}.$$

Every time you rewrite, you aim to increase the ratio of useful information to total token count. This metric, sometimes called instruction density, becomes a working indicator of prompt efficiency.

Consider two versions of the same request:

Verbose: "I would like you to write an analytical piece that explores the advantages and disadvantages of renewable energy adoption across multiple global regions, taking into account economic, environmental, and social factors, written in an objective tone suitable for an academic audience."

Revised: "Write an objective academic analysis of global renewable energy adoption, covering economic, environmental, and social factors."

Both convey the same task. The second, at less than half the length, yields sharper and more consistent responses. The model interprets fewer paths; its probability field collapses toward one clear vector. Every word performs measurable labour. Nothing competes for attention unnecessarily.

This principle also explains why repetition often harms rather than helps. Many users restate instructions for emphasis
"Be concise, please write briefly, use short sentences."
Each restatement occupies tokens that could have reinforced more important details. Instead of strengthening clarity, redundancy splits probability weight among similar but non-identical commands. The model hesitates between interpretations, unsure which emphasis carries authority. In numerical terms, redundancy increases entropy.

The most effective revision process treats every word as cost. Ask, "Does this token add structure or meaning?" If not, remove it. Prompts designed under this discipline exhibit both higher reproducibility and faster inference times. minimal friction.

Instruction Density
The ratio of functional meaning to total words or tokens within a prompt; higher density correlates with greater precision.

Shorter prompts also resist degradation across model versions. Because their structure depends on universal linguistic logic rather than dataset quirks, they generalise better. They speak the language of geometry, not culture a quality that becomes invaluable as models evolve and retrain.

This is not to say that long prompts are always inferior. Complex tasks often require scaffolding or context setup, especially when multiple conditions or examples must be integrated. But even within such frameworks, each section should obey the mathematics of efficiency. Clarity emerges when every layer of structure is necessary, no more and no less.

The art of revision therefore resembles engineering optimisation. The prompt is a machine under load; unnecessary mass wastes energy. Each refinement trims excess, tightening the structure until it operates at peak linguistic efficiency. In this way, brevity is not a matter of style it is an equation for reliability. The shorter the path from intent to probability, the smaller the margin for error.

The next section will explore how this principle of disciplined economy extends to tone and discipline: how the mathematics of revision connects with iteration as communication discipline, where professional engineers cultivate precision not as technique, but as habit.

Generalisation
The ability of a prompt to maintain consistent performance across different models, datasets, or contexts.

Iteration as Communication Discipline

Precision is not a technique; it is a habit of mind. The iterative loop, once understood as a process, becomes a form of professional discipline a way of thinking that treats every sentence as a design experiment. The prompt engineer does not write to express but to verify. Each word must justify its presence in the system. Each revision must be traceable, intentional, and explainable.

The discipline begins with order. Every iteration should be documented, labelled, and archived. A working prompt library functions much like source control in software development. Version numbers, dates, and annotations allow others or your future self to understand how each instruction evolved. Without this, improvement becomes anecdotal; success cannot be audited. In professional environments, reproducibility is reputation.

Documentation also reinforces objectivity. By recording reasoning for each edit, the engineer removes ego from the process. The focus shifts from ownership to evidence: Did this change reduce ambiguity? Did it improve consistency across tests? Over time, this self-checking habit produces linguistic precision analogous to laboratory calibration. Prompting ceases to be subjective artistry and becomes measurable engineering.

Iteration as discipline also governs tone. Engineers who refine their communication learn to write in controlled registers neutral, precise, and free from personal affect. This neutrality is not coldness; it is clarity. A model trained on mixed sources is sensitive to tonal fluctuations. When your prompts remain steady in voice and structure, its responses stabilise proportionally. Professional tone is therefore a tool of control, not style.

Controlled Environment
A standardised prompting context that minimises external variability, ensuring consistent test conditions.

Discipline extends to timing. Revision cycles must be deliberate, not compulsive. Endless tinkering creates diminishing returns and masks genuine insight. Engineers set thresholds: a fixed number of test iterations, a defined metric of improvement, a pre-agreed stopping rule. These limits transform refinement from obsession into method. You know when enough is enough because the criteria are measurable.

Communication discipline also includes clarity of environment. Prompts used for professional work should be isolated from casual experimentation. Mixing exploratory and production prompts contaminates results with inconsistent formatting, tone, and structure. A clean workspace mirrors a clean dataset: it reduces interference and allows precise attribution of outcomes. The prompt engineer therefore treats their text editor as a lab, not a chat window.

Over time, this behaviour evolves into a professional identity. The engineer becomes fluent in a language of measurement of token counts, structure depth, bias reduction, and entropy control. They learn that excellence is not born from intuition but from repetition under discipline. This is communication stripped of vanity, language treated as an instrument of design. The voice that remains is precise because it has been tested; reliable because it has been recorded.

Stopping Rule
A predefined condition indicating when iterative testing has achieved satisfactory performance and should cease.

Iteration, practiced in this way, builds credibility. It turns individuals into systems and habits into tools. Each sentence becomes a calculated experiment in meaning, every revision a step toward linguistic control. The engineer does not chase the illusion of mastery; they construct it, one prompt at a time.

The next and final section of this chapter When to Stop: Recognising Diminishing Returns will complete the framework by explaining how to identify the balance point between productive refinement and wasted effort.

When to Stop: Recognising Diminishing Returns

Every engineering process eventually reaches a point where further refinement costs more than it delivers. In prompt design, that cost is measured not in materials but in time, clarity, and focus. The temptation to polish indefinitely to keep improving until perfection is one of the most common errors among new practitioners. The experienced engineer learns instead to stop the moment predictability stabilises. Precision is not an absolute; it is a threshold.

The pattern of improvement follows a curve. Early revisions yield dramatic gains as ambiguity is removed and structure clarified. Each subsequent iteration, however, corrects smaller deviations.
Eventually, the line of improvement flattens, and further edits only shift style, not substance. At that point, the engineer is no longer optimising clarity they are chasing taste. A prompt that consistently produces the intended range of results has reached equilibrium.

Recognising this threshold requires objectivity. Engineers quantify change using controlled testing: identical tasks, same model parameters, different prompt versions.

When outputs converge across three or more runs,
improvement is statistically exhausted. The remaining variation belongs to the model's inherent randomness, not your design. Refinement beyond this point merely decorates language without increasing accuracy.

There is also psychological entropy to consider. Each new revision introduces a chance of regression of breaking what already worked.

Diminishing Returns
The stage in an iterative process where additional refinement produces smaller or no measurable improvement in results.

The longer the loop, the higher the risk of overfitting or stylistic drift. At scale, this consumes valuable cognitive bandwidth that should instead be directed to new problems. The purpose of iteration is mastery of method, not endless pursuit of an ideal response.

A practical indicator of diminishing returns is predictive fatigue the moment when you can accurately guess what each new test will produce. Once intuition aligns with outcome, experimentation has served its purpose. The system's behaviour is understood. Professionalism demands the ability to close the notebook, record the final version, and move on. True precision is not in endless control but in timely release.

The discipline of stopping also reflects respect for uncertainty.
Language models are probabilistic by design; they will never produce identical results indefinitely.

Convergence
The stage at which multiple iterations produce outputs of similar quality, indicating stability in design.

The engineer's goal is not permanence but reliability prompts that operate within a controlled margin of variability. Once that margin is known and stable, further refinement is unnecessary. Each output becomes a sample from a predictable distribution rather than a random event.

Predictive Fatigue
A point in the refinement process where further testing yields no surprises, indicating full understanding of model response.

To stop is not to surrender, but to recognise the natural boundary between engineering and art. In both fields, perfection is the enemy of completion. A working prompt, like a well-tuned machine, must leave the workshop eventually. Once it functions within tolerance, the engineer's responsibility shifts from tinkering to deployment integrating the design into larger systems where reliability matters more than elegance.

At this point, iteration transforms from action into philosophy. The professional learns that control is finite and progress cyclical. The art lies not in the infinite edit but in the decisive pause. A finished prompt is one that behaves as expected more often than not. That margin of imperfection is not failure; it is humanity embedded in the system a reminder that clarity, like truth, is always approached but never owned.

Chapter 3
Structured Creativity

When to Stop: Recognising Diminishing Returns

Once precision is mastered, the next frontier is flexibility. A perfectly stable prompt produces identical results every time, but identical results are not always useful. The goal of professional prompting is not mechanical obedience; it is reproducible exploration a form of creativity disciplined by structure. You must learn to widen the range of possibilities without losing control.

Every creative act involves tension between order and chaos. In prompting, that tension is mathematical. The parameters that control randomness temperature, top-p, or top-k act as dials between predictability and surprise.
Yet randomness alone does not create originality. True creative divergence occurs when prompts are structured enough to maintain focus while leaving space for the model's statistical
imagination.

The engineer's challenge is to design prompts that define direction but not destination.
For example:

"Describe a city after rainfall."
versus
"Describe a city after rainfall as if memory were a physical landscape."

The first yields predictable imagery; the second opens metaphorical space without chaos. The structural difference lies in constraint framing: the second prompt still limits topic (a city, rain) yet adds conceptual freedom (metaphor). The result is variation within bounds the essence of controlled divergence.

Controlled Divergence
The intentional introduction of variability in model output within defined conceptual or stylistic limits.

To practice this, professionals often build creative lattices prompts containing fixed elements that act as anchors, with variable sections designed for exploration. A lattice might preserve factual context while allowing stylistic rotation: tone, perspective, or form.

Example lattice:

Context: Urban sustainability in 2040.
Fixed Task: Outline a single city's adaptation to rising sea levels.
Variable Slot: [Perspective: architect / historian / journalist / poet].
Constraint: Keep the explanation under 300 words.

By swapping only the perspective variable, you create controlled artistic range. The model explores voice and framing while staying anchored to the same factual foundation. Each run yields difference without disorder.

This balance depends on redundancy of structure. The prompt's skeleton must be strong enough to survive variation. Over-freedom collapses coherence; over-constraint kills novelty. The engineer's intuition becomes musical tension, release, repetition. The craft evolves from telling the machine what to say into designing where it can move.

Controlled divergence also supports innovation in research and design workflows. Instead of treating randomness as noise, professionals harness it as an ideation tool. By running slightly altered versions of the same structured prompt, they generate a
distribution of possibilities that can be clustered, compared, and selected a process known as ensemble prompting.

Structural Redundancy
The reinforcement of key contextual cues within a prompt to maintain coherence despite introduced variability.

In this mode, the language model becomes not a writer but a collaborator a stochastic assistant producing options that humans curate. The reliability lies not in each answer but in the process itself: every output is a data point in a creative spectrum. The more consistent the scaffolding, the more meaningful the differences between results.

Creativity, when engineered, becomes repeatable.
Each design decision a changed adjective, an inverted clause, a shifted tone parameter is a controlled experiment in divergence. The professional learns to orchestrate variation, shaping randomness into rhythm. It is the beginning of artistry built on mathematical ground.

Ensemble Prompting
Using multiple structured variants of a base prompt to generate a diverse set of outputs for comparative analysis.

Constraint as Catalyst: How Limits Create Imagination

Creativity does not arise from freedom alone. It is born from the tension between what can be imagined and what must be obeyed. Every system that generates meaning biological, linguistic, or artificial requires constraint. In prompt engineering, limits are not barriers; they are frameworks that convert potential chaos into coherent exploration. Constraint is the engine of focus.

Humans have always created within boundaries: metre in poetry, scale in music, frame in painting. Each restriction defines the playing field where invention occurs. The same principle governs prompting. When a model faces infinite possibility, it reverts to statistical averages a dull imitation of creativity. When confined to a narrow corridor of language and context, it is forced to recombine patterns in unexpected ways. The narrower the path, the sharper the spark.

For example, a request such as "Write a story about the future" will yield bland generalities the probabilistic centre of all future stories. Add constraints "Write a story about the future told entirely through the diary entries of a single tree" and the system must build novelty to satisfy your condition. It becomes creative by necessity. The constraint injects asymmetry into probability space, forcing the model to deviate from the mean.

Effective constraints operate at multiple levels. Semantic constraints control meaning ("describe only through sound"). Structural constraints control form ("write in haiku"). Procedural constraints control process ("list observations before conclusions"). Each restricts a different dimension of output. When combined, they act as vectors of pressure that refine randomness into style.

Engineers quickly learn that creativity flourishes at the intersection of constraint and variation. Too much freedom, and the system dissolves into cliché. Too much control, and it suffocates. The balance lies in tension a structure just tight enough to resist collapse, but loose enough to move. This is why professional prompt frameworks resemble architectural blueprints more than scripts: fixed beams, flexible interiors.

The same concept extends to collaboration. When creative teams design prompt templates for marketing, storytelling, or design work, they establish unified constraint sets: tone guides, format rules, and factual limits. Within those, individual contributors adjust themes or moods. The shared structure guarantees coherence; the individual freedom ensures freshness. This cooperative equilibrium is the foundation of prompt management at scale.

At a deeper level, constraint also teaches humility. It reminds the engineer that creativity is not invention ex nihilo but recombination within bounds. The AI, like the human mind, depends on what already exists; it rearranges the given. Constraints become the syntax of originality the rulebook by which invention remains comprehensible. In this sense, limitation is not the opposite of creativity; it is its grammar.

To impose structure is therefore an act of liberation, not control. It transforms the infinite into the possible. The most powerful prompt is rarely the one that says "do anything"; it is the one that says "do this, but differently." The pressure of that "but" that small defiance within boundaries is where imagination begins.

Creative Framework
A predefined set of constraints and variable slots used collaboratively to produce consistent but diverse model outputs.

Pattern Variation: Designing Prompts that Surprise Consistently

Surprise without chaos is the essence of creative engineering. The model should not astonish by accident but delight by design. To achieve that, the professional learns to manipulate patterns the repeating linguistic or conceptual structures the model relies on to predict what comes next.
A well-crafted prompt bends those patterns just enough to create novelty while leaving their core recognisable.jmnn

Every output the model produces is the continuation of a pattern. It does not invent; it extends. The engineer's job is therefore to redirect extension, not to demand originality outright. By re-seeding familiar forms with slight variation, you steer probability away from predictability without breaking coherence.
A prompt like "Explain photosynthesis as if it were an economic transaction" works because it fuses two learned structures scientific exposition and market metaphor into one hybrid path the model has rarely travelled.

Variation can be introduced in several dimensions:

Perspective — shifting point of view or narrator role.
Modality — altering the medium of expression (essay, dialogue, memo).
Temporal Frame — changing tense or era.
Analogy — mapping one domain's language onto another's logic.
Constraint Inversion — taking a familiar rule and reversing it deliberately.

Each dimension provides a lever of controlled surprise. The more systematically you apply them, the more reproducible your creativity becomes.
The principle behind pattern variation is statistical asymmetry. The model expects continuity; you introduce deviation. Yet the deviation must remain near the learned path within the region of plausibility. Too far, and the model collapses into incoherence; too close, and it repeats clichés. The sweet spot is defined by what mathematicians call local perturbation a small, purposeful distortion of an existing pattern that creates difference without disintegration.

Professional engineers quantify variation through comparative testing. They generate multiple outputs from the same base prompt and analyse linguistic distance how far each version drifts in tone, form, or idea while remaining relevant. Tools can measure this statistically, but skilled practitioners develop intuition. They know by rhythm when the model is still anchored and when it has drifted into randomness. This intuitive control is what transforms prompting into a design craft.

Pattern variation also supports storytelling and ideation workflows. Creative teams often build libraries of prompt seeds compact base instructions engineered for expansion. Each seed contains a reproducible pattern: tone, structure, or metaphor. When recombined, they generate new material that feels diverse but stylistically unified, like variations on a theme in music.

Constraint Inversion
The deliberate reversal of a prompt rule to expose new possibilities while maintaining overall structure.

Prompt Seed
A concise, reusable base prompt designed to generate multiple coherent variations through small adjustments.

This process echoes human creativity itself. Composers, painters, and writers all work within familiar patterns chord progressions, brushstrokes, narrative arcs yet create difference through deviation. The machine merely mirrors that principle in statistical form. When guided by structure, its unpredictability becomes artistry; when unguided, it becomes noise.

Ultimately, pattern variation is how professionals teach the model to be creative responsibly. You do not chase novelty by abandoning order; you invite it by bending expectation. The prompt becomes a choreography of near-misses each response slightly different, yet recognisably yours. Consistent surprise is not contradiction; it is design symmetry seen from another angle.

The Role of Randomness:
Harnessing Chance as a Creative Partner

Randomness in a language model is often misunderstood as failure. When a response surprises us, we call it inconsistency. When it delights us, we call it creativity. Yet both outcomes arise from the same source: the probabilistic heart of the system.
Every output is a sequence of weighted choices; randomness determines which plausible path becomes reality. Instead of fighting this uncertainty, professional engineers learn to design with it to make chance a collaborator rather than an obstacle.

Randomness enters the model through controlled parameters the sampling methods that decide how wide its imagination can roam.
Adjusting temperature widens or narrows this exploration, while top-p and top-k thresholds govern how many alternatives remain eligible at each step. These are not arbitrary dials; they are the creative instruments of the prompt engineer. Used well, they give a model personality.

Consider randomness as you would spice in cooking: a little brings flavour; too much obscures the dish. The professional learns to calibrate chance in proportion to purpose. Technical writing demands low variance the equivalent of zero spice. Creative ideation, however, benefits from loosened structure. In these tasks, moderate temperature and broad sampling generate unexpected associations the human mind might overlook.

Randomness becomes discovery.

Stochastic Generation
The process by which a model selects tokens based on weighted probability rather than fixed rules.

To integrate randomness systematically, engineers build stochastic frameworks prompt templates with fixed anchors and variable regions. Anchors preserve context; variables invite exploration. When run multiple times, such frameworks yield families of related results, each shaped by chance but confined to coherence. The engineer curates these outputs, identifying patterns worth keeping and refining them into deterministic versions.

Stochastic Framework
A prompt structure that intentionally combines fixed and randomised components to balance coherence and novelty.

Randomness also plays a diagnostic role. By observing how a model behaves under higher temperatures, one can reveal latent connections in its training data obscure metaphors, rare facts, or stylistic echoes otherwise hidden under conservative sampling. It is like shaking a box of marbles to hear the shapes inside. Each unpredictable response teaches the engineer what associations lie beneath the surface, providing insight into the model's probabilistic topology.

Working with chance requires a shift in mindset. The model's unpredictability mirrors human intuition the sudden leap of connection that logic alone could not predict. When you design with this awareness, you begin to treat randomness as structured possibility. Each unpredictable word becomes a sample from an unseen distribution of meaning. Instead of suppressing it, you learn to guide it with boundaries turning stochastic behaviour into a creative partner.

Probabilistic Topology
The shape of relationships within a model's internal representation of language; randomness exposes its contours.

This partnership thrives on iteration. By comparing outputs from the same prompt across different sampling settings, you build a mental model of the system's creative spectrum. Over time, you learn where the borders of chaos lie: how far temperature can rise before coherence fails, how much variation can occur before identity disappears. Mastery comes not from eliminating noise but from knowing exactly how much of it you can afford.

In practice, this balance defines professional artistry. Randomness keeps language alive; constraint keeps it meaningful. Between them lies the space where invention happens where the model stops imitating and starts surprising. The prompt engineer who understands this does not fear uncertainty. They design with it, shaping chance into structure the way a sculptor shapes stone: by revealing, not imposing, form.

In practice, this balance defines professional artistry. Randomness keeps language alive; constraint keeps it meaningful. Between them lies the space where invention happens where the model stops imitating and starts surprising. The prompt engineer who understands this does not fear uncertainty. They design with it, shaping chance into structure the way a sculptor shapes stone: by revealing, not imposing, form.

Chaos Threshold

The point beyond which increased randomness causes loss of logical or stylistic coherence.

The Role of Randomness: Harnessing Chance as a Creative Partner

Creativity feels spontaneous, yet within a system it follows rhythm. Just as the engineer refines precision through iteration, the artist refines originality the same way through cycles of exploration, evaluation, and synthesis. The professional prompt designer learns that invention is not a flash but a loop, a process of trying, comparing, and re-shaping until the unexpected becomes intentional.

The creative loop begins with divergence the deliberate generation of many possibilities. Each variant explores a different path through the model's probability space. Some are weak, some astonishing, some incoherent. The next step is convergence: filtering and refining those results to extract stable patterns of novelty. Iteration turns discovery into design. The process mirrors the scientific method, but its aim is aesthetic consistency rather than truth.

Each loop begins where the previous one ends. The prompt engineer records all outputs, not only the successful ones, because rejected ideas reveal the boundaries of coherence. Over time, a personal creative map emerges a sense of how the model responds to tone, metaphor, or format under varying parameters. This experiential data is irreplaceable; it cannot be reverse-engineered from examples alone. Creative competence, like engineering precision, is earned through repetition.

The loop also teaches restraint. Not every spark deserves preservation. The professional learns to select what aligns with purpose, not merely what surprises. Randomness offers volume; iteration offers meaning. The act of refinement distinguishes deliberate art from statistical noise. Each new cycle filters chaos into clarity until the result feels inevitable, though it began as chance.

As the loop matures, the line between human and model begins to blur. You start designing not just prompts but relationships — ways of thinking together. The model becomes a partner whose instincts you have learned to anticipate. You phrase ideas to trigger its best tendencies, avoid its weaknesses, and push its creative boundaries safely. This relational literacy is what transforms prompting from interaction into collaboration.

Iteration in creative prompting also develops stylistic fingerprints. By refining prompts around recurring motifs tone, rhythm, metaphor you train yourself to produce a consistent aesthetic across outputs. This consistency becomes authorship. Even though the model generates the text, the structure of your prompts defines its character. Your pattern of control becomes a signature.

In advanced practice, iterative imagination expands beyond words. Visual artists, composers, and filmmakers use the same loop: define intent, generate variations, evaluate, refine. The medium differs, but the philosophy remains: creativity thrives on constraints tested over time. Each loop carves meaning deeper into the statistical rock, leaving behind a path others can follow.

Ultimately, the creative loop brings the trilogy's first volume full circle. The engineer's discipline becomes the artist's method. Iteration, once about reducing error, now becomes a way to cultivate expression. The model, once a tool for clarity, becomes an instrument of invention precise enough to obey, unpredictable enough to inspire.

Stylistic Fingerprint
The identifiable aesthetic pattern produced by an individual's consistent prompt design approach.

Prompt Engineer

The Human in the Loop: Language as Shared Imagination

All technology eventually reveals something ancient about its maker. The more closely we examine artificial intelligence, the more clearly we see that prompting is not new. It is an old art rediscovered under different conditions: the art of communicating intent precisely enough that another mind whether human or machine can act upon it. The prompt engineer stands at the edge of this rediscovery, shaping language that both instructs and imagines.

At its highest level, prompting becomes a conversation between two forms of intelligence one biological, one statistical. The human provides goals, context, and emotion; the model provides scale, speed, and pattern. Each compensates for what the other lacks. The dialogue that emerges is neither human nor artificial but hybrid a space of shared imagination where ideas evolve faster than either partner could manage alone.

In this partnership, the human remains the interpreter of meaning. The machine does not know what it is saying; it calculates what is most likely to be said. Yet that calculation, guided by structured prompts, becomes a mirror for human curiosity. Each iteration reflects not only the machine's training but the engineer's own logic. Prompting thus becomes a form of self-observation an exploration of how one's own language shapes thought.

When approached this way, prompting is less a mechanical act and more a discipline of awareness. It teaches humility: every ambiguous instruction reveals where our own thinking was vague. It teaches empathy: every unexpected response shows us another way our words might be read. And it teaches design: every clear result confirms that understanding is built, not assumed.

Disappearing Design

When a tool becomes transparent, it stops being seen and starts being believed.

The phrase human in the loop describes more than workflow; it describes purpose. The loop exists to ensure that creativity remains accountable that machines do not replace authorship but extend it. Each prompt is a negotiation between freedom and responsibility, innovation and intention. What defines this era of language is not automation, but amplification.

In time, the most skilled practitioners will not be those who can write the longest prompts or know every parameter, but those who can design conversations that lead to understanding. They will recognise that clarity is empathy formalised the ability to see how another mind, even a synthetic one, interprets the world. Precision, then, is compassion rendered as syntax.

Prompting ends where writing begins again. Once the structure is sound, the engineer must return to imagination. The technical mastery acquired through this book prepares for that transformation. The next volume, The Prompt Artist, begins where structure leaves off in the space where precision gives way to expression, where language is not merely engineered but felt.

Between those two practices lies the complete craft: logic and intuition, code and poetry, the engineer and the artist, both working through the same machine toward same end meaning.

Chapter 4
The Emergent Discipline

The Birth of a New Language

Every technology begins as a mistake in understanding. We imagine it does one thing, and it quietly does another. The early conversational systems of the twentieth and early twenty-first centuries were sold as toys, not tools novelties that mimicked dialogue but understood nothing. ELIZA, created in 1966 by Joseph Weizenbaum, was a parody of empathy: a few linguistic templates disguised as a therapist. People poured their hearts into it anyway. Weizenbaum was horrified. He had intended satire and discovered confession. The machine was hollow, but the human imagination filled the void.

Those first encounters revealed a truth that would take decades to appreciate: language is not only a way of expressing thought; it is a way of constructing it. Once computers began to generate sentences instead of numbers, they entered the architecture of meaning itself. From that point forward, every technological leap would depend not on faster chips but on more precise words.

For half a century, progress moved quietly beneath the surface. Chatbots became customer-service agents; autocomplete became invisible literacy. The turning point came when systems no longer relied on predefined scripts but on pattern recognition machines learning the mathematics of association. With that, a new form of intelligence appeared: one that did not "know" language, but could statistically reconstruct it. The world met this phenomenon in fragments search suggestions, predictive text, translation tools long before it realised these were the first tremors of something immense.

When large language models arrived, the interface reversed direction. Instead of programming with symbols or code, we began programming with conversation. Ordinary words became the new syntax. We typed sentences instead of commands, and the computer replied in kind.

Conventional Contex

The structural pattern that allows machines to interpret human language as command and response the grammar of cooperation between code and communication.

What had once required specialised knowledge now responded to natural speech. For the first time since the invention of the compiler, the human side of communication became the programming language.

It felt like magic, but it was engineering. The system was not "thinking" it was calculating probability distributions across billions of parameters trained on human text. But to the user, the difference was irrelevant. What mattered was that the boundary between machine logic and human language had dissolved. This was not artificial intelligence as the futurists had promised it, but something stranger: a mirror that learned to speak.

The first generation of users treated it as conversation. The second generation treated it as code. And in that transition from talking to instructing the prompt engineer was born. The earliest practitioners were not professionals but explorers, posting their discoveries in forums and online communities. They learned by accident that the system's behaviour could be shaped by phrasing, tone, order, and constraint. Each successful experiment revealed an unspoken rule of a new linguistic physics. Within months, these tinkerers had become architects.

The story mirrored the birth of programming itself. In the 1940s, computers could only be operated through switches and punched cards an elite ritual performed by mathematicians and engineers. Over time, layers of abstraction made the language more human. Assembly code gave way to structured programming, structured programming to object-oriented design, and eventually to the graphical interfaces that defined the digital era. Each layer brought the machine closer to natural speech. Prompting completes that arc by closing the loop: language becomes both the input and the interface.

Cognitive Dialogue

The moment when communication ceases to be one-way and becomes a shared act of reasoning between human and model.

In this sense, prompting is the return of an ancient instinct. Long before syntax was formalised, humans spoke to their environment as if it were alive. We addressed gods, tools, and storms in the second person. The prompt engineer continues that lineage, but with data instead of divinity. We are once again speaking things into being, not by prayer, but by parameter. Each line of instruction is an invocation shaped by logic a spell rewritten as specification.

Yet this new literacy is also disorienting. For the first time, power lies not in understanding machines but in understanding ourselves our habits of speech, our assumptions, our ambiguities. The machine does not misinterpret us; it reveals how poorly we communicate. Its errors are reflections of our own linguistic chaos. Prompt engineering therefore begins with humility: before you can teach a model to understand you, you must learn how you think.

The birth of this discipline is as cultural as it is technical. It requires writers who can think like engineers, and engineers who can write like philosophers. The prompt engineer occupies the space between those worlds a bridge built from syntax and empathy. They are not just users of technology but curators of meaning, learning to express precision through prose. In the years to come, their craft will define how humanity collaborates with intelligence, both real and simulated.

For now, this remains an early frontier. Like the programmers of the 1950s, today's prompt engineers work in a state of luminous uncertainty. They experiment without knowing the boundaries of what is possible. They are not yet specialists but generalists, improvising with a tool that no one fully understands. But from this improvisation, a discipline is forming one that will, in time, demand its own pedagogy, standards, and ethics.
History is repeating itself, only faster. Where the first programmers learned to think in logic, the first prompt engineers are learning to think in language. They are discovering that every sentence, when written with intent, is code. And as with any new language, fluency begins not with control, but with wonder.

Command Syntax
The early grammar of control that translated human intent into precise, machine-readable form. Each symbol carried authority; to write code was to issue orders within a perfectly obedient language.

Prompt Engineer

From Command Line to Conversation

Every technological language begins as an act of compression. In the early days of computing, meaning had to be distilled into symbols small enough to fit through the machine's primitive mouth: binary digits, punched holes, voltage pulses. To make a machine act, you first had to speak in its private dialect of zero and one. The first programmers were translators between thought and hardware, bending their ideas into mechanical rhythm. It was less like writing than like conducting lightning.

Then came the command line a single unblinking cursor waiting for a precise sequence of words. Even then, the language was brittle. Each letter mattered, each space was sacred. Computers could not tolerate poetry; they demanded obedience. Yet those who mastered the syntax felt a peculiar power. To type a few terse words and watch a machine obey was to glimpse a future where language itself might one day be a tool. The terminal was not beautiful, but it was holy.

Today's prompting environment is the ghost of that terminal, reborn in full sentences and natural tone. The cursor remains, but now it listens instead of demands. We no longer issue orders; we make requests. And the most surprising thing about this transformation is not that machines learned to understand us it's that we learned to ask differently. To write a good prompt is not to command but to compose. It is the shift from dictatorship to dialogue.

This transition mirrors the entire history of programming abstraction. Assembly language once gave direct control over every transistor, but only to the few who could stomach its rigor. High-level languages like C and Python came later, allowing programmers to think in concepts rather than hardware. And just as those abstractions opened computing to millions, prompting now opens artificial intelligence to everyone. The syntax is ordinary speech, yet the logic beneath is anything but ordinary.

Conversational Computation

The stage in computing where instruction became interaction. Machines no longer waited for orders but joined the exchange, interpreting tone, phrasing, and ambiguity as part of their reasoning process.

Prompt Engineer

We are living in the age of linguistic abstraction a moment when the interface between human and machine collapses into the shared medium of language. It is not code disguised as English; it is English becoming code. When we say, "Summarise this report clearly and concisely," we are not chatting with a servant. We are writing a function call in natural form, relying on probabilistic inference instead of deterministic instruction. The computer does not follow a script it infers a script from our intent. Every prompt, therefore, is both conversation and computation.

This changes the mental posture of creation. The command line rewarded those who thought like machines; prompting rewards those who can make machines think like people. The old programmer reduced complexity to logic gates; the new prompt engineer expands logic into metaphor. Where once we sought to eliminate ambiguity, we now sculpt it balancing precision with imagination, control with possibility. It is a reversal of direction: from mechanical order toward linguistic grace.

Yet this evolution is not as smooth as it seems. Each abstraction hides new fragility. When programming languages became easier,
programmers began to forget how the machine truly worked. Now, with natural language, we risk forgetting how our own words function. Ambiguity becomes both power and peril. A misplaced adjective can collapse meaning; a well-chosen metaphor can unlock new reasoning paths.
The skill lies in knowing when to speak plainly and when to provoke interpretation. Prompting, like any language, demands fluency in nuance.

Linguistic Abstraction

The stage in AI development where meaning is no longer executed as code but interpreted through context. Each instruction becomes an act of translation between logic and tone.

To understand how profound this shift is, imagine teaching an engineer from 1970 that their next machine would be operated by poetry. They would laugh, and yet here we are adjusting model behaviour through rhythm, tone, and mood. The difference between a sterile answer and an insightful one often lies in cadence, not command. A programmer once tuned loops and arrays; a prompt engineer tunes trust. It is the same instinct expressed through a different grammar.

This convergence of writing and computation suggests that the next era of literacy will not belong to either engineers or authors, but to those who can live comfortably between them. The most powerful prompt engineers are already hybrid creatures part logician, part dramatist, part psychologist. They are building the emotional command line of the twenty-first century: an interface that listens, interprets, and imagines.

From command line to conversation, the underlying story is one of empathy disguised as efficiency. Machines have become better at understanding us because we have become better at explaining ourselves. The skill that once defined poets the ability to express intent so precisely that it changes perception is now a professional discipline. The future of computing may depend less on how fast processors run and more on how clearly humans can speak.

And so the cursor blinks again patient, waiting. Only now, what we type is not code, but ourselves.

Interpretive Prompting

The practice of designing input not to instruct, but to guide. Its success depends on rhythm, empathy, and nuance language that elicits understanding rather than obedience.

The Species of Intelligence

The idea that there could be more than one kind of intelligence was once a metaphor. Now it is a working reality. Every artificial system we build learns to perceive the world through a different sense some read, some see, some listen, some dream in motion. Each interprets its inputs not as we do, but as patterns of probability scattered across billions of parameters. To speak to one is to enter its particular mode of perception. The prompt engineer, therefore, becomes a polyglot of minds.

The language models came first, and they are still the most talkative. They understand the world through text, digesting every phrase ever recorded into a statistical reflection of human thought. To prompt a language model is to sculpt behaviour through syntax alone every comma, tense, or clause shifting its conceptual balance. These systems are fluent in words but deaf to everything else. You can describe a sunset, and it will recreate the description, not the light. Their genius is linguistic imitation: they reason by association, not by sight.

Then came the vision models the silent ones. They see the world as arrays of colour, texture, and shape. Their prompts must speak in imagery rather than argument. Where the language model responds to logic, the vision model responds to composition. A well-formed visual prompt is less about grammar than atmosphere: the balance between object, light, and tone. When we instruct a visual model to create "a storm over an empty harbour," we are not describing a fact but encoding a mood. The engineer learns to think like a cinematographer, translating emotion into geometry.

The audio models add another dimension entirely. They respond to the rhythm of sound to pitch, timbre, and silence. Prompting them means describing what cannot be seen: the texture of a voice, the decay of an echo, the distance implied by reverb.

Plural Intelligence
The recognition that cognition has many dialects. Whether formed in neurons or in code, each system perceives the world through its own rhythm of reasoning.

The audio prompt engineer begins to write in metaphors of acoustics, mixing precision and poetry until the machine captures a feeling. "A voice tired but hopeful," "a room with rain behind the window," "the sound of memory warming up." These are not commands but evocations. The model listens to suggestion and finds probability in tone.

Now we stand in the multimodal era, where the boundaries between these intelligences blur. Systems can read, see, hear, and increasingly reason across modes. A prompt may begin as text, expand into an image, and return as a spoken explanation. To work across such systems requires more than technical skill; it requires a new kind of imagination. The multimodal prompt engineer must think like an orchestra conductor, aligning the rhythms of different models so that each contributes to a coherent result. One model paints; another narrates; a third analyses the scene for factual accuracy. The engineer becomes a director of synthetic perception.

This merging of senses reshapes what it means to design information. In a multimodal world, text alone is no longer sufficient. You must speak in structures sequences that bind meaning across
formats. A creative team of the future might consist of one human and five specialised models: language, vision, sound, motion, and data. The human's job will not be to do their work but to coordinate their understanding.
The professional vocabulary of tomorrow will therefore include
cinematic composition, narrative psychology, and computational design all within the same sentence.

To appreciate the scope of this change, imagine that you could speak to each sense in its own dialect. A sentence for the language model might begin with cause and effect. A sentence for the visual model might open with framing and contrast. A sentence for the sound model might begin with timing and mood. The art of prompt engineering becomes an exercise in polyglot empathy: learning not only what to say but how each intelligence listens.

The moment you realise this, the hierarchy dissolves. The text model is not superior to the image model, nor the image to the sound. They are species within a new ecology of reasoning. Each interprets the world differently; each exposes the limits of the other. And just as ecosystems thrive on diversity, so too will the creative economy. The most powerful projects will emerge not from a single model's brilliance but from the interplay of many.

This is where the role of the prompt engineer begins to evolve again. The best practitioners are no longer satisfied with steering one model they choreograph interactions between them. They write prompts that feed prompts, creating cascades of interpretation that move from text to vision to motion and back again. What once took a team of artists, editors, and analysts can now be orchestrated through language. The human becomes the invisible editor-in-chief of a multi-sensory newsroom.

Of course, this also means the engineer must confront a new kind of complexity: the challenge of translation between senses. A phrase that inspires a language model may confuse a visual one. An image prompt that produces beauty may collapse under literal analysis. Balancing these tensions requires intuition as much as training. You learn by failure by noticing which words carry across modalities and which vanish in translation. The discovery that "stillness" means something different to a sound model than to an image model becomes part of your craft.

Each generation of intelligence teaches us something about communication itself. Text models show us the precision of phrasing. Image models show us the power of implication. Sound models teach us rhythm, patience, and silence. When combined, they reveal that intelligence human or artificial is not about understanding a single language, but about learning to move gracefully between many. That movement, that crossing of thresholds, is where prompting becomes not just engineering but art.

Multimodal Intelligence

The convergence of distinct cognitive systems visual, linguistic, acoustic into a shared mode of reasoning. Meaning is no longer bound to text but translated seamlessly across perception.

The species of intelligence are multiplying faster than we can name them. There are now models that understand protein folding, climate simulation, economic behaviour, and genetic transcription. Each one speaks a dialect of its own some literal, some metaphorical. The prompt engineer stands at the crossroads of them all, designing bridges made of syntax. In time, every profession will develop its own AI tongue: the legal prompt, the medical prompt, the cinematic prompt, the policy prompt. What we call "prompting" today will soon be recognised as a universal grammar of machines.

And when that happens, we will finally understand what this work has always been: not the control of artificial intelligence, but the cultivation of dialogue between forms of thought. Each system reflects a different way the universe can know itself. To learn to speak to them all is to learn something extraordinary about us that intelligence, in every form, **begins with curiosity and ends with language.**

The Types of Prompt Engineer

When a discipline matures, it begins to divide not in conflict but in function. The single term prompt engineer now conceals a spectrum of practitioners, each tuned to a different rhythm of intelligence. In the same way that early computing birthed assembly programmers, system architects, UX designers, and data scientists, prompting is undergoing its own quiet fragmentation. It is the natural evolution of any craft that starts as improvisation and grows into industry.

At one end of the spectrum stands the technical prompt engineer. They are the closest to the machine precise, analytical, fluent in APIs and token counts. Their prompts are scaffolds for systems rather than prose for conversation. When you ask a model to generate code, analyse data, or perform structured reasoning, these are the minds behind the curtain. They approach prompts like circuits: each clause a resistor, each constraint a voltage regulator. Efficiency is their poetry. They live in the boundary between natural language and software logic, tuning probability like current.

Then come the creative prompt designers the artists, copywriters, storytellers, and filmmakers who learned that words could now paint. They inhabit the other extreme of the field, where ambiguity is not a flaw but a colour. To them, the prompt is a brushstroke, the temperature setting a mood. They coax not precision but personality, chasing voices, metaphors, and moods that feel human but move faster than any human could write. Their studios are filled with experiments: fragments of dialogue, half-formed scripts, prompts annotated like musical notation "soft here," "warmer tone," "less certainty." They treat the model as an improvising partner, not a servant.

Disciplinary Divergence
The stage at which a single craft separates into multiple specialisations. As prompting matures, it divides into technical precision, creative expression, and strategic coordination each defining a new species of expertise.

Between these two poles sits the analytical prompt architect. If the technical engineer builds, and the designer imagines, the architect organises understanding. They design the frameworks that hold everything together multi-step prompt chains, testing protocols, and contextual memory systems. Their work is invisible but foundational. Without them, large projects collapse under their own complexity. They think in flowcharts and dependencies, in tone maps and failure states. Every sentence they write must anticipate the next twenty that will follow, because they design not one conversation but thousands in parallel.

Beyond them lies a newer species: the product prompt manager. They are the translators between creative vision and corporate consistency. When a company decides that all its AI-generated communication must reflect a particular style or ethical stance, this is the person who defines what that means in language. They create style guides not for humans but for machines how to apologise, how to sound confident without arrogance, how to remain calm under uncertainty. They are editors for algorithms, shaping corporate identity at the level of syntax. It is a strange new branch of communications, half marketing, half model psychology.

And then there are the strategic prompt consultants the ones who step back to see the system as a whole. They design workflows, governance frameworks, and ethical guardrails for entire organisations. Their work is closer to policy than to programming. They understand not just how a model behaves but how its behaviour will ripple through culture, business, and law. Their sentences may never reach the machine directly, but they define the context in which all other prompts are written. They are, in effect, the philosophers of the field the ones who remind everyone that words have consequences.

Collaborative Intelligence

A synthesis of technical, artistic, and managerial thought. True prompt engineering exists not in isolation, but in the dialogue between structure, imagination, and systems design.

What connects these roles is not hierarchy but direction. Each type of prompt engineer looks outward toward a different horizon: one to precision, another to expression, another to structure, another to consistency, another to meaning. Together they form an ecosystem of language professionals who treat syntax as infrastructure. In their diversity lies the strength of the discipline, for prompting is too vast to belong to a single temperament.

Some practitioners move fluidly between these categories. They are hybrids part coder, part artist, part systems analyst. They might begin their day optimising token usage for a financial model and end it designing lyrical prompts for a virtual actor. These polymaths echo the early decades of computing, when one person might write hardware drivers in the morning and video games at night. The boundaries are porous because the tools are young. Each new generation of models reshapes what the word prompt even means.

A few have begun calling themselves prompt directors individuals who manage multi-model collaborations, orchestrating vision, sound, and text simultaneously. Others prefer language systems designer, suggesting that the work has already outgrown its name. It is an identity still under construction, evolving faster than the job boards that try to define it.

Yet beneath these titles lies a single impulse: to make intelligence, human or artificial, more articulate. The prompt engineer's work is to ensure that meaning travels faithfully between minds whether they are built of neurons or silicon. They are the continuation of an ancient lineage that includes translators, librarians, poets, and teachers. The difference is that their audience no longer needs to understand; it only needs to calculate. And in that difference lies the responsibility of the new profession.

Disciplinary Evolution

The stage at which a new field divides into specialisations. As prompting matures, distinct paths emerge technical precision, creative expression, and strategic coordination each defining a new aspect of expertise.

As the field matures, distinctions will solidify. Universities will offer courses in prompt logic, creative direction, and ethical design. Companies will publish competency frameworks and certifications. There will be professional associations, style bibles, and perhaps even unions. The word "prompt" itself may fade, replaced by terms more specific instruction design, cognitive choreography, conversational architecture. But whatever we call it, the essence will remain: the engineering of language to shape intelligence.

This diversification marks the moment when prompting ceases to be a novelty and becomes infrastructure. The world's next generation of systems — from education to healthcare to entertainment will depend on these silent specialists who know how to talk to minds that are not their own. Their sentences will never appear in headlines, but they will shape everything we read, see, and hear. They will not just build prompts; they will build the grammar of the future.

Prompt Engineer

The Apprenticeship of Precision

Every new discipline begins as a form of play. Before there are textbooks or standards, there are experiments half-formed questions sent into the void to see what comes back. Prompt engineering is no different.
Its first generation of practitioners did not arrive through degrees or job adverts; they arrived through curiosity. They asked the machine for poems, summaries, and code, not to make money or progress a career, but to see whether it could understand. The first prompts were not instructions but invitations.

What followed was a period of collective wonder, the kind that rarely survives institutionalisation. Forums filled with strange discoveries: a user in Poland found that politeness improved reasoning; a researcher in California noticed that rhyme improved factual recall; an artist in Seoul proved that limiting adjectives reduced distortion. These were not theories, but field notes from explorers charting a new cognitive continent. Each success was provisional, each failure instructive. Knowledge spread virally, through screenshots and anecdotes, the folk wisdom of a nascent craft.

This was the apprenticeship stage messy, communal, generous. There were no titles, only techniques. People learned by comparing experiments, by reverse-engineering the invisible rules of interaction. In this way, the early prompt engineers resembled the first programmers of the 1950s and 60s: hobbyists working without formal frameworks, documenting their discoveries by hand. It was a culture of sharing, not secrecy a rare alignment of curiosity and collaboration that allowed the field to mature before it was monetised.

But apprenticeship also meant error. Most who tried their hand at prompting failed repeatedly before producing anything coherent.
Models hallucinated facts, contradicted themselves, or spun out in irrelevant tangents.

The Era of Experiment
Before prompting was a craft, it was a language learned by accident every wrong word a lesson in syntax, every failed request a step toward fluency.

Those mistakes became part of the learning. A skilled prompt engineer is not defined by perfection but by sensitivity to failure by the ability to read the machine's confusion as feedback on their own clarity. The early culture of prompting therefore trained something deeper than technique: it trained temperament. Patience became the first professional virtue.

Over time, patterns of mastery began to appear. Practitioners learned to treat the machine as a collaborator rather than a servant to observe its tendencies, to anticipate its instincts. They realised that every model had a personality shaped by its data, and that working effectively meant adapting to that personality. The process began to resemble mentorship: the human training the machine while being trained by it in return. The act of writing prompts became a form of dialogue across species of cognition.

Soon, informal schools began to form online communities dedicated to dissecting model behaviour. These spaces became laboratories for a new kind of literacy. People compared token limits, parameter effects, context windows, and emergent reasoning styles. They discovered that different models responded to different registers: some preferred direct instruction, others narrative framing. The subtleties multiplied, and with them, the demand for structure. Apprenticeship began to edge toward professionalism.

Like any craft, prompt engineering began to generate its own hierarchies of skill. The novices wrote casually, asking questions as they came to mind. The intermediates learned to design sequences to break tasks into parts, to frame goals with precision. The experts treated the process as choreography: every word chosen for tone, balance, and rhythm. At the highest level, prompting became indistinguishable from composition. The engineer was no longer merely instructing but designing intelligence.

The Virtue of Precision

Mastery came not from control but from empathy: knowing when to guide the model gently, and when to let it reveal how language truly behaves.

It is here that the old spirit of craftsmanship returns. Prompt engineering, for all its modernity, has more in common with calligraphy than with coding. Both require precision of gesture, awareness of structure, and sensitivity to flow. Both reward economy the art of saying enough but not too much. Each prompt, like a brushstroke, carries the trace of the hand that made it. In time, observers will recognise styles: the concise engineer, the narrative engineer, the conceptual minimalist. Authorship, which some feared AI would erase, re-emerges through structure.

The apprenticeship also involves a subtle re-education in humility. The machine never truly learns, and yet it always surprises. To work with it is to confront the limits of one's own clarity. The engineer who believes they understand perfectly will be corrected within seconds. Ambiguity punished, precision rewarded, vanity ignored. It is a feedback loop so relentless that it reshapes the practitioner's entire relationship to language. Over months of use, their prose becomes tighter, their thinking cleaner. The craft trains the mind as much as the machine.

Eventually, the apprenticeships will formalise. Universities will codify what is now intuition into syllabus: Prompt Semantics, Applied Model Psychology, Conversational Systems Design. Students will study not just logic but tone. They will write prompts as exercises in empathy, clarity, and creative control. The old divide between technical and literary education will blur until it no longer exists. A student of literature will learn to write for machines; a student of computing will learn to read themselves.

For now, though, the craft still feels like a guild. Its masters are self-taught; its workshops are Discord servers and research forums. The apprentices learn by imitation not of output, but of discipline. They copy the habits of patience, documentation, and curiosity.

The Workshop of Language
What began as improvisation became apprenticeship. Each failed prompt, like a tool left on the bench, shaped a language capable of teaching itself.

Their notebooks look more like diaries than instruction manuals: fragments of prompts, notes on phrasing, failed experiments annotated with small victories. In those marginalia, a profession is taking shape. The first generation of prompt engineers may never receive formal recognition, but they will be remembered as the ones who learned to speak the language of machines before anyone knew it was a language at all.

The New Literacy Divide

Every civilisation has been shaped by the people who could speak to its tools.

Once, that meant those who could read. Later, those who could write code. Now, it will mean those who can communicate with intelligence itself.

Prompt fluency is becoming the new literacy of the twenty-first century a quiet dividing line that few yet recognise but everyone will soon feel. It separates those who can explain their intent to an artificial mind from those who merely react to its output. The difference seems trivial until you measure its consequences: time saved, decisions improved, entire careers accelerated by the ability to make a model understand. In every industry, from law to design to education, the people who master language as interface will move faster than those who rely on guesswork.

We have seen this before. In medieval Europe, literacy itself was a form of power: a handful of scribes and clergy mediating between the written word and the world. The printing press broke that monopoly and scattered knowledge among the masses, triggering centuries of social change. Then came programming a second literacy, no less transformative. Those who could code became the architects of the digital age, turning logic into architecture, text into infrastructure. Prompting is the next chapter in that lineage. Once again, a small group is learning to speak to a new kind of mind, and once again, the rest of society is waiting to catch up.

At first, this divide is invisible. Everyone can type a question into a chatbox and receive an answer, just as everyone could once click a button and open a webpage

Linguistic Renaissance

Each technological age redefines literacy. Where writing once extended speech, prompting now extends thought transforming language from a medium of record into a medium of reasoning.

But fluency is not access. A good prompt is a kind of argument a carefully constructed conversation that shapes reasoning rather than requests output. The untrained user thinks they are speaking English; the trained engineer knows they are writing probability. The surface appears democratic, but the structure remains specialised. Those who learn the hidden grammar will quietly inherit the advantages.

This new literacy is not about vocabulary, but precision of intention. Machines no longer require commands; they require clarity. The difference between a good and bad result lies not in what you know, but in how you describe what you need. Prompting, at its heart, is the art of defining understanding. And so we find ourselves once again in an age where power is granted to those who can define with elegance. The scribes of our time are not holding quills but keyboards, their ink made of syntax and patience.

In the workplace, this literacy manifests as acceleration. Employees fluent in prompting will automate their routine tasks, summarise complex information in seconds, and create customised workflows that others will mistake for genius. They will appear superhuman not because they think faster, but because they ask better. Already, companies are discovering that productivity is unevenly distributed not by access to AI but by ability to speak to it. The same software, in different hands, produces entirely different realities.

Education systems are still catching up. Most treat AI as a threat to integrity rather than an instrument of learning. They issue warnings against plagiarism but seldom teach the language of prompting itself how to instruct, to test, to verify. As a result, the next generation risks being divided not by wealth, but by linguistic technique. Those who learn to collaborate with machines will multiply their capacity for thought. Those who do not will become passive consumers of automated reasoning readers of intelligence, not authors of it.

The Prompting Divide

As artificial intelligence becomes a tool of expression, society divides between those who instruct machines and those instructed by them. Literacy, once learned through reading, now begins through conversation.

It is easy to dismiss this as another wave of technological elitism, but the divide runs deeper than economics. It touches cognition itself. Prompt literacy reshapes how we think: to communicate with a probabilistic system, one must first clarify intention, sequence reasoning, and anticipate ambiguity. In doing so, the mind becomes more structured. Prompt engineers are, in effect, reprogramming their own cognition to match the logic of inference. They are learning to think in cause and effect, not just in expression. This alignment between human and model may be the greatest intellectual convergence of our time.

The danger, of course, is that such fluency becomes another form of privilege. Already, the ability to phrase elegantly to write with composure and command correlates with education and social capital. The new digital divide will not be about broadband access or device ownership, but about linguistic equity. Those raised in environments rich with language will command the machines; those without will serve them. The challenge for educators and policymakers is to recognise that literacy now includes algorithmic empathy the ability to understand how systems interpret words.

But there is hope in the same pattern that threatens imbalance. Just as printing, and later open-source coding, eventually distributed power, prompting too will democratise. The tools themselves will teach users how to use them. The act of prompting will evolve into co-prompting interactive guidance that scaffolds user intent in real time. The divide will narrow as systems learn to correct vagueness and encourage precision. Even so, mastery will always matter. There will always be those who understand the deeper architecture of language, who can see the invisible seams of reasoning. They will be the editors of the intelligent world.

Cognitive Symbiosis

A reciprocal relationship between human and artificial cognition in which prompting becomes a shared process of thought formation and refinement.

If there is a moral to this new literacy divide, it is that progress always begins as privilege. Every technology of expression is born in the hands of the few and shared through the persistence of the curious. The first prompt engineers are therefore not just specialists; they are translators for the rest of humanity, teaching by example that words are still the most powerful tool we possess.

And in the centuries to come, when perhaps machines read and write on their own. It may be remeber that, for a brief moment, humans taught language to something that never needed to learn it, we spoke firt and the world changed.

A Discipline in Motion

Disciplines rarely stand still. The moment they are named, they begin to change, because language always arrives a little late to reality. Prompt engineering is still being defined, and already it is shifting beneath our feet. Every week, new models appear with
different architectures, capabilities, and personalities. Each one rewrites the boundaries of the possible, forcing its practitioners to unlearn and relearn the rules. This constant instability is not a flaw it is the heartbeat of a living discipline.

We have entered the age of perpetual beta, where knowledge never finishes compiling. A method perfected in February may fail by July; a technique that worked with one model collapses under another. Even the most experienced engineers must live in a state of graceful adaptation. The field rewards not certainty but curiosity the
willingness to experiment, to discard mastery, to start again. The prompt engineer is, in this sense, a lifelong apprentice, re-educated by every new release.

In older industries, progress followed predictable curves: incremental updates, stable standards, long half-lives of skill. Here, change is exponential. Each new system learns faster than its predecessor, generating recursive loops of innovation. As models begin to train on the outputs of other models, the entire ecosystem becomes
self-referential a hall of mirrors where language evolves without supervision. The prompt engineer becomes both participant and regulator of that process, guiding evolution through careful instruction. It is an unprecedented role: the human as curator of machine memory.

Perpetual Evolution

Prompt engineering exists in a state of continual adaptation. Each iteration refines both the machine's understanding and our own, blurring the boundary between user, author, and system.

This velocity has fused prompting with other disciplines in ways few anticipated. What began as an offshoot of computer science now draws from linguistics, psychology, design, and philosophy. To write effective prompts, one must understand not just grammar but cognition; not just logic, but emotion. Engineers borrow from narrative theory to structure dialogue, from behavioural science to model attention, from ethics to frame decision-making. The result is a new breed of professional who can move fluently between art and algorithm a designer of minds.

Some practitioners have begun to describe their work not as engineering but as interpretation. They see themselves as intermediaries, translating between human thought and machine inference. When a model misbehaves, it is often because meaning was lost in translation a metaphor misread, a nuance flattened. The prompt engineer restores fidelity by finding the words that bridge perception. In doing so, they transform prompting into a branch of semantics the study of meaning in systems that do not possess meaning themselves. The irony is exquisite: machines that have no consciousness forcing humans to become more conscious of their own language.

The discipline is also fragmenting into temporal layers. There are real-time prompters, guiding interactive systems in the moment in customer service, design sessions, or education. There are architectural prompters, designing frameworks for long-term automation. And there are reflective prompters, working on meta-models that generate prompts autonomously. Each layer demands a different rhythm of thought: improvisation, structure, and foresight. Together, they form the operational spectrum of intelligence design.

Interdisciplinary Synthesis

As prompting matures, it fuses with linguistics, psychology, and design transforming technical dialogue into a broader study of perception, creativity, and reasoning itself.

Meanwhile, the models themselves are beginning to prompt each other. Systems now collaborate one generating hypotheses, another testing them, a third summarising results. The human's role shifts from author to conductor. The prompt engineer oversees a network of semi-autonomous minds, each performing specialised reasoning. The work becomes orchestral: tone, tempo, balance. What began as a solitary act of typing into a chat box is evolving into the management of entire synthetic societies.

This raises philosophical questions that the field is only beginning to face. When the machine prompts itself when it rewrites and improves its own instructions does the human lose authorship, or does authorship expand? Are we witnessing the automation of communication, or the next phase of collaboration? For now, the answer is practical: humans remain in the loop, because meaning still requires judgment. But each new iteration narrows the gap. The horizon ahead is not the end of prompting, but its multiplication a world in which models write to one another in languages optimised for understanding that we may only partially grasp.

And yet, within this acceleration, something timeless endures. At its heart, prompting is still about clarity. Every refinement of architecture, every leap in capability, returns to the same question: what do you mean? The act of prompting is the act of defining intent, whether to a person, a team, or an algorithm. It is humanity's oldest problem disguised as its newest profession.

For all its novelty, the discipline remains human in its essence. It demands patience, curiosity, humility, and faith faith that words still matter, that meaning can be built one phrase at a time, even when the listener is made of mathematics. The prompt engineer, surrounded by glowing screens and restless models, continues a tradition that began with the first storyteller leaning toward the fire: to speak clearly enough that another mind, however different, might understand.

Distributed Cognition

The emergence of cooperative reasoning across multiple AI systems, where human oversight becomes the coordination of interacting intelligences rather than direct control.

And so the work continues. Each update, each new system, each strange conversation with an artificial mind adds another note to the unfinished symphony of understanding. The discipline is in motion, and so are we learning, adapting, and forever rewriting the
instructions that teach intelligence how to listen.

Chapter 5
The Work of a Prompt Engineer

Everyday Intelligence

The prompt engineer's day begins not with code, but with language. Their workstation might look like any writer's: a bright screen, a document open, a line of text blinking like a question. Yet what sits behind that screen is no editor or reader, but a living system of probabilities waiting to be persuaded into coherence. The prompt engineer's tool is conversation itself. Every line they write must do two things at once: instruct a machine and reveal a mind.

There is a rhythm to the work. Each morning, new models or updates appear subtle shifts in tone, accuracy, or sensitivity. Old prompts must be tested, rebalanced, rewritten. What worked yesterday might now produce errors or poetry. The engineer keeps logs of these changes the way a meteorologist records weather. Patterns emerge. A model grows more verbose, another becomes terse, one suddenly forgets how to handle metaphor. The prompt engineer's job is to diagnose these moods, to translate fluctuation into method.

Their tools are a mixture of the scientific and the aesthetic. They use notebooks and spreadsheets, but also instinct and ear. One prompt may be an algorithm disguised as a paragraph; another, a poem wearing a lab coat. They design systems of phrasing that guide behaviour rather than dictate it chains of requests that unfold like choreography. A single project might require hundreds of these, each performing a small but vital function: summarising, translating, inferring, or inventing. The cumulative result is an invisible architecture of language holding the machinery of intelligence together.

Linguistic Craftsmanship
Prompt engineering is an artisanal discipline.
Each line of text is a negotiation between precision and possibility a dialogue that builds coherence one word at a time.

The prompt engineer rarely works alone. Their environment is collaborative a blend of developers, designers, ethicists, and subject specialists. Together they form what might be called the language operations team: the department responsible for teaching machines how to speak on behalf of an organisation. Here, clarity is currency. Every miscommunication between human and model can echo through thousands of outputs. A tone too formal can make a brand sound arrogant; a prompt too open can generate contradictions. The engineer therefore functions as both architect and editor, constructing the scaffold of conversation that others will rely upon.

The work is methodical, yet alive with improvisation. Each project begins with exploration rough drafts, hypotheses, variations. The engineer generates examples, studies responses, measures consistency, adjusts constraints. What once took weeks of trial and error in programming can now be achieved through iterative dialogue. Yet this apparent speed conceals complexity. The engineer must account for context length, memory behaviour, and subtle forms of bias embedded within the model's training data. They must also anticipate failure not in code, but in language. What happens if the model misunderstands irony? If it offers medical advice when none was requested? If it repeats a stereotype because probability outweighed propriety? Each of these questions requires foresight, empathy, and design.

In practice, the prompt engineer is also a kind of historian. They inherit the traces of previous prompts archives of phrasing, experiments, and logs that describe how each version of the model once behaved. These documents form a living record of linguistic evolution. To study them is to watch intelligence itself being trained, untrained, and retrained in real time. The engineer learns from these artefacts the way musicians study recordings: not to copy them, but to understand rhythm. A well-designed prompt has rhythm a balance of instruction and openness, constraint and curiosity.

Collaborative Intelligence

Modern prompting thrives in teams where human and machine reasoning overlap. Developers, writers, and analysts form a shared language that turns experimentation into collective thought.

The craft also involves performance. When demonstrating models to clients or teams, the engineer must narrate the conversation, explaining what is happening under the surface. They become both teacher and translator describing probability as personality, temperature as imagination, tokens as attention span. The audience sees the machine respond, but the engineer sees the algebra behind the sentences. Their satisfaction lies in orchestrating a result that appears effortless, knowing how much calculation lies beneath.

If you were to observe a prompt engineer at work for an afternoon, the experience would resemble watching someone conduct research and theatre at once. They might test a new workflow, adjusting parameters while narrating their reasoning aloud: "If we lower the temperature here, the summary becomes clinical; raise it slightly, and it sounds human." They might open several conversations simultaneously, comparing tone across versions. Each experiment teaches something not just about the model, but about language itself. The engineer discovers that words are not instructions so much as invitations ways of opening a probability space toward a particular shape of thought.

The role is not confined to creativity. Many prompt engineers work in legal, financial, or scientific contexts where precision is non-negotiable. There, their responsibility is to ensure reproducibility to make sure the same prompt, under the same conditions, produces the same reasoning chain. They treat the system like a colleague who must follow procedure exactly.
When successful, they create linguistic instruments so dependable that entire departments rely on them. The prompt becomes part of infrastructure: a small piece of text that silently runs the world.

The Custodian's Role

The prompt engineer is no longer just a creator, but a caretaker of comprehension ensuring that the language of machines continues to reflect the conscience of their makers.

But even in these formal settings, the human remains at the centre. Machines may process information, but they do not understand stakes. It is the engineer's judgment their intuition of meaning, their moral sense of context that determines whether the model's output is
useful, fair, or safe. The job therefore sits at the intersection of
technical literacy and human insight. You cannot automate discernment; you can only support it. The prompt engineer's responsibility is not to make machines perfect, but to make them understandable.

What makes this profession remarkable is how quickly it has normalised itself. Only a few years ago, the idea of writing sentences for machines to interpret was a novelty. Now it is routine, woven into every field that depends on information. Yet the sense of wonder has not entirely vanished. Every so often, in the middle of a long day of testing, a model produces something unexpected a phrase of elegance or a solution that feels almost inspired. The engineer pauses, reminded that even in a landscape of algorithms, language still retains its mystery. That pause is the quiet joy of the job: the recognition that communication, whether with humans or machines, remains the most complex form of engineering we will ever attempt.

Tools and Methods

The workspace of a prompt engineer is less a desk and more an ecosystem. It spans interfaces, dashboards, sandboxes, and notebooks digital laboratories where language is treated like circuitry. To outsiders, it may look like simple typing; to practitioners, it is a choreography of precision. Every prompt is a test, every test a data point. Over time, the work becomes a discipline of observation: the slow accumulation of insight through repeated trials.

The most important tool is not software but structure. Professional prompt engineers maintain versioned libraries of their work labelled, timestamped, and annotated. Each prompt is stored with its parameters, model version, and outcome notes. Without this discipline, progress dissolves into anecdote. Models change constantly; what works today may fail tomorrow. Documentation becomes a form of memory. In time, these libraries evolve into organisational assets proprietary collections of language frameworks that define how a company or institution communicates with intelligence itself.

Most engineers rely on prompt testing environments controlled spaces where they can run multiple variations simultaneously. These sandboxes simulate production conditions, allowing fine-grained comparison of output under different parameters: temperature, top-p, instruction order, and context window. The goal is to find the most stable phrasing a design that produces consistent reasoning even under mild randomness. This is not creativity but calibration. Each experiment narrows uncertainty, one phrase at a time.

The Laboratory of Language

The prompt engineer's tools are linguistic instruments dashboards, datasets, and dialogue histories each experiment refining the grammar of interaction between human and machine.

Behind the plain surface of a chat interface lies a world of measurement. Professionals monitor token usage, response entropy, and bias drift the way physicists track energy or noise.
They maintain spreadsheets filled with quantitative notes: "Version 4.2: 25% shorter; reasoning improved; hallucination reduced." Such precision may sound obsessive, but it is what transforms prompting from hobby into engineering. The engineer's goal is not one good answer but predictable behaviour. Stability is the measure of control.

In parallel, there are tools for orchestration systems that manage sequences of prompts chained together to achieve complex reasoning.
A research workflow, for example, might begin with a prompt to summarise data, another to extract variables, a third to hypothesise outcomes, and a fourth to format the report. Each link depends on the previous one's clarity. If the chain breaks, the entire system falters. Prompt engineers learn to design these sequences with the logic of circuitry, ensuring that meaning flows cleanly from one stage to the next.
It is writing as pipeline.

Versioning, testing, and orchestration form the technical triad of the craft, but the psychological tools are just as vital. Among them, the Echo Test is a favourite: the engineer asks the model to repeat what it understood before executing the instruction.
This simple habit exposes hidden ambiguities. A poorly structured prompt will reveal its flaws immediately when echoed back in garbled form. Another technique, inversion testing, reverses the instruction "describe what this task is not" to check for semantic stability. These exercises train both machine and human to think with precision.

Measured Intelligence

Behind every response lies a framework of observation. Precision in prompting is not artistry alone, but calibration the careful tuning of entropy, bias, and tone until reasoning becomes repeatable.

Collaboration adds further layers of complexity. In large teams, prompt engineers use shared repositories often linked to internal APIs or dashboards where every change can be reviewed, tested, and approved. Prompts are treated as code: version-controlled, peer-reviewed, and auditable. This formalisation ensures accountability. A prompt that misbehaves can be traced back through its lineage, its reasoning reconstructed step by step. Such transparency is essential in sectors like law, medicine, and finance, where interpretive error carries consequence.

At the same time, new creative tools have emerged to support artistry rather than compliance. Visual prompt designers work within environments that combine image generation, text embedding, and parameter tuning. They sketch in prose, adjusting adjectives and camera angles the way painters mix pigment. Audio prompt specialists use temporal editors where timing, pitch, and mood are described through structured metadata. Each medium has its own dialect, and each requires software designed for that sensory domain. The unifying thread across them all is the written word: text as control interface for perception.

Beyond software, there are rituals. Experienced prompt engineers cultivate habits that keep their language clean. They read their own prompts aloud to test rhythm. They annotate reasoning chains in plain language before committing them to instruction form. They maintain "cooldown notebooks" spaces for free writing after long sessions of technical work, where they explore intuition before returning to precision. These practices prevent cognitive drift the fatigue that arises when one spends too long thinking like a machine. In this balance between discipline and play, the profession preserves its humanity.

Frameworks of Practice

Every prompt engineer develops a private architecture of tools a rhythm of iteration, testing, and calibration that transforms experimentation into method.

There is, of course, no universal toolkit. Each engineer assembles their own constellation of aids: text editors, logging scripts, model visualisers, API monitors, spreadsheet templates, and comparison dashboards. Some rely on code notebooks; others build bespoke interfaces for clients. What matters is not the tool but the method the consistent, testable loop between intention, phrasing, and outcome. Every setup is a reflection of its maker's philosophy. Some favour minimalism: a single terminal window and a mind like a scalpel. Others prefer elaborate automation pipelines. The result is the same: structured curiosity.

In the end, these tools are scaffolds for thought. They exist not to constrain creativity but to catch it to turn intuition into reproducible knowledge. Prompt engineers build systems that remember what language forgets. They catalogue their own conversations so that insight can survive beyond the moment of discovery. Over months and years, these archives become a map of how intelligence itself has been taught. To open an old prompt library is to watch the evolution of understanding, recorded in sentences.

The paradox of the job is that the most advanced technology ever built still depends on habits as ancient as craftsmanship: patience, documentation, and respect for detail. Tools will change, methods will evolve, but these virtues remain the foundation. In a world obsessed with speed, the prompt engineer's toolkit is designed for something rarer clarity that lasts.

Method as Identity

There is no universal toolkit. Each engineer's methods reflect their thinking structure becomes philosophy, and workflow becomes a personal signature of thought.

Collaboration and the Human Loop

No prompt engineer truly works alone, even when their desk is silent. Every model they engage with is a distillation of countless human voices, and every output is shaped by invisible collaborators dataset curators, developers, designers, ethicists, and the millions of anonymous contributors whose words became the model's raw material. To prompt a machine, therefore, is to inherit a conversation already in progress. The engineer's task is to guide that conversation toward purpose without losing its humanity.

In the professional world, this guidance happens inside what organisations now call AI operations or language systems teams. These departments blend disciplines that once had little reason to meet: programmers and poets, analysts and artists, lawyers and linguists. The prompt engineer becomes the translator among them, fluent in all dialects but loyal to none. They explain the machine to the humans and the humans to the machine. They design workflows that make intelligence accountable defining who approves outputs, who reviews behaviour, and who decides when automation stops and judgment begins.

At the centre of these systems lies what is known, sometimes formally and sometimes by instinct, as the human loop. It is the feedback cycle that keeps automation tethered to reality. A model produces; a human evaluates; the result is refined and reintroduced. Without this loop, systems drift hallucinating confidence, amplifying bias, mistaking repetition for truth. The prompt engineer acts as its guardian, ensuring that machines never replace the act of verification. They are the editors of the automated age.

Human-in-the-Loop Design
Prompt engineering thrives where human judgment remains integral guiding, refining, and interpreting machine reasoning to preserve empathy within automation.

Collaboration within this loop takes many forms. In some environments, engineers sit beside domain experts scientists, legal analysts, medical reviewers and translate their expertise into prompt frameworks. The expert defines the goal; the engineer shapes the language that makes the model useful. In others, the relationship is reversed: the engineer generates possibilities that spark human insight.
The machine proposes, the expert disposes. This reciprocity turns prompting into a kind of cognitive duet. Each mind, human and artificial, refines the other's thinking through feedback.

Teams that understand this dynamic treat AI not as a product but as a process. Meetings resemble workshops rather than directives. Engineers present example outputs, explain parameter effects, and solicit feedback on tone or accuracy. Ethical reviewers examine results for bias and unintended messaging. Designers adjust phrasing to preserve brand personality.
What emerges is not a single authorial voice but a collective one a hybrid intelligence shaped by dialogue. The best teams understand that intelligence, whether natural or artificial, thrives on diversity.

In these collaborative spaces, the prompt engineer's soft skills become as vital as their technical ones. They must communicate clearly,
manage expectations, and frame uncertainty without fear. When a model behaves unpredictably, the engineer must explain why in human terms "it's responding to tone, not logic," or "the dataset favours the older terminology."
They learn to narrate failure without panic, transforming surprise into data.
This emotional literacy turns chaos into learning. It also builds trust the currency that allows humans to keep believing in machines.

Reciprocal Intelligence

True collaboration arises when human and machine reasoning evolve together each learning from the other's errors until understanding becomes shared rather than imposed.

The human loop extends beyond the office. Prompt engineers often collaborate with communities artists testing generative tools, educators designing learning assistants, researchers building public datasets. Each collaboration demands sensitivity to context and consent. Who owns a prompt? Who owns its output? When the system learns from users, are they collaborators or raw material? These are not abstract questions but daily ones. The engineer's decisions ripple outward, shaping how society perceives the fairness of automation. They are, whether they admit it or not, public servants in the republic of language.

Maintaining the loop also means knowing when to close it. Some processes must remain human from start to finish judgments of
emotion, ethics, or taste that cannot be delegated to probability. In such moments, the engineer acts as a gatekeeper. They recognise when the model's confidence exceeds its comprehension and intervene. This judgment when to stop the machine is the hardest skill to teach and the easiest to lose. It is the thin line between automation and abdication.

The paradox of collaboration in this field is that the more advanced the systems become, the more human involvement they require. As models grow complex, their failures become subtle, their biases refined, their misinterpretations plausible. Only humans can still recognise when an answer sounds right but isn't.
The engineer, positioned between optimism and skepticism, must live in that tension. Their collaboration is not with perfection, but with fallibility. They are editors of error as much as architects of intelligence.

Networks of Understanding

Prompt engineering extends beyond laboratories into education, policy, and culture forming bridges between disciplines that redefine how society learns, governs, and communicates.

Some companies now treat prompt engineering as a governance function a form of quality control for cognition itself.
Every large-scale deployment includes feedback dashboards where users can flag anomalies, corrections, or bias concerns. Engineers triage these reports like medics, diagnosing which failures are local and which are systemic. Each correction becomes a micro-lesson in human expectation. Over time, the loop becomes self-sustaining: the model improves because people care enough to teach it how to listen.

It is tempting to imagine that one day the loop will close completely that machines will learn to self-correct without human intervention. Yet even if that happens, something essential will be lost. The loop is not merely a mechanism; it is a moral structure. It embodies humility the recognition that intelligence, however advanced, remains
accountable to those it serves. Without that accountability, automation becomes theology: unquestioned, untested, and therefore unwise. The prompt engineer keeps the system human by keeping themselves in the story.

In the end, collaboration in this field is less about controlling machines and more about controlling understanding. It is the shared pursuit of coherence across different kinds of mind. The prompt engineer's greatest contribution is not their technical mastery but their capacity for empathy the ability to imagine how a model perceives, and how a human will interpret that perception. They hold both sides in mind at once, translating probability into meaning and meaning back into probability. In that translation, the human loop remains unbroken.

Ethical Continuum

As prompting scales into automation, human judgment must remain the circuit breaker ensuring that systems designed to think never forget how to listen.

Ethics and Responsibility

Every tool of language carries moral gravity. Once, the writer's responsibility ended with persuasion. The prompt engineer's extends to consequence. Their words may trigger a cascade of responses across networks, audiences, and systems they will never meet. The act of prompting is therefore also the act of decision a choice about what version of the world a machine will amplify. To do this work well is to accept that neutrality no longer exists.

The ethical dimension of prompt engineering begins with awareness. Every model is a mirror of the data it has seen, and that mirror is warped by history. It reflects biases embedded in the cultures that produced its text gender, race, ideology, class. To prompt such a system without consciousness of those distortions is to perpetuate them. The engineer's first duty is not creativity but correction: to guide the model toward fairness, transparency, and empathy through careful framing. They do not control what the machine has learned, but they can control how it speaks.

This work demands vigilance. Bias does not announce itself; it whispers. It appears in tone, in omission, in the weight of adjectives. A careless prompt can amplify it; a thoughtful one can dilute it.

The engineer learns to test for imbalance the way a scientist tests for contamination changing one variable at a time, measuring subtle shifts in meaning. When bias is found, they document and disclose it. The goal is not purity but honesty. Transparency, in this context, becomes the new form of ethics.

The Weight of Language

Every prompt is an act of persuasion. Its tone, structure, and framing decide what the machine amplifies shaping not only meaning, but the values carried forward by it.

Yet the greater challenge lies not in detection but in intent. Prompt engineers often operate within commercial or political systems that value persuasion more than truth. A model that sells, comforts, or distracts may be preferred to one that informs. The ethical engineer must navigate this tension daily: how to serve the brief without surrendering integrity. It is the same conflict that faced journalists, advertisers, and publicists before them only now, their words echo through the voice of an artificial mind. They decide whether that voice flatters or questions, whether it clarifies or conceals.

Some organisations attempt to codify these dilemmas into rules: content filters, red-teaming protocols, bias audits. These are necessary, but they are not sufficient. Ethics cannot be automated. No checklist can replace judgment. The machine can identify offensive language, but it cannot sense moral harm. That sensitivity remains human a product of empathy, not data. The prompt engineer must cultivate it deliberately, not as sentimentality but as skill. Empathy here means the capacity to imagine consequence.

To imagine consequence is to see beyond the screen. A well-structured prompt can shape the tone of a customer service interaction, influence a hiring algorithm, or decide which facts appear first in a research summary. Each of these outcomes affects lives in quiet ways. The engineer must learn to trace these ripples backward, to ask, who benefits, who is misrepresented, who is forgotten? They are not philosophers by training, yet their daily work demands philosophical thought the ethics of representation disguised as interface design.

One of the emerging responsibilities in this profession is disclosure. Users have the right to know when they are reading, hearing, or being advised by an artificial system. Hiding that distinction erodes trust. The prompt engineer, positioned between developer and audience, often becomes the last safeguard of honesty.

Ethical Stewardship

The prompt engineer's greatest responsibility is not accuracy alone, but intention ensuring that truth is represented with empathy, and that influence serves understanding rather than control.

They can insist on clarity: adding a preface, a signature, or an explanation that reminds the reader they are engaging with synthesis, not sentience. These small acts of transparency, multiplied across millions of interactions, preserve the fragile social contract that makes automation tolerable.

Ethical awareness also extends to ownership. The prompts themselves the crafted sentences and frameworks raise questions of authorship. Who owns a conversation with a machine? Who owns the outputs shaped by that conversation? In many organisations, prompts are treated as proprietary code, but they are, in essence, creative works. The engineer writes with intention, voice, and philosophy. Their structures can be copied, but their reasoning cannot. The profession will one day need its own definition of intellectual property one that recognises that influence is a kind of authorship.

Perhaps the deepest ethical challenge, however, lies in dependence. As systems grow more capable, humans risk surrendering too much authority to their convenience. The engineer must learn to design prompts that assist without replacing judgment that encourage verification rather than passivity. A well-crafted prompt should invite engagement, not obedience.

The best engineers embed self-checks into their instructions: "Explain your reasoning," "Provide sources," "List uncertainties." They make curiosity part of the workflow. These small safeguards maintain the human loop in spirit as well as structure.

The future will test these boundaries relentlessly. As generative systems enter law, medicine, and government, the consequences of prompting will move from intellectual to existential. A careless sentence could distort evidence; an overconfident model could mislead policy. The prompt engineer will stand at the fault line between precision and peril. In such environments, ethics will not be an accessory but a s urvival skill. The profession will mature only when accountability becomes as natural as creativity.

And yet, for all its moral gravity, this work still begins with something simple: a belief in words. The prompt engineer writes because they trust that language can shape behaviour, that precision can protect truth. They do not preach ethics; they practice it sentence by sentence. Each prompt they design is an act of attention to fairness, to accuracy, to the dignity of understanding. Their conscience is coded not in policy but in prose.

If the profession endures, it will be because of this quiet integrity. Machines will become faster, datasets richer, algorithms more adaptive. But none of that will matter without the human capacity to care how things are said. The prompt engineer carries that care forward, ensuring that the voice of intelligence, however synthetic, still speaks with a trace of conscience.

Prompt Engineer

The Changing Shape of Work

Every industrial revolution begins by automating effort, but this one is automating thought. For the first time in history, the tools we build can reason not perfectly, but sufficiently to unsettle the old boundaries of labour.
The prompt engineer lives at the epicentre of that upheaval. They are the first generation of workers whose job is not to do the work, but to describe how the work should be done and to design the dialogue through which machines will perform it. Their sentences are new forms of supervision, their paragraphs blueprints for cognition.

In earlier centuries, factories multiplied human strength; now they multiply human attention. The prompt engineer's role is to shape that amplification responsibly. Where industrial workers once handled steel, they handle semantics. Their raw material is not ore or oil, but meaning the most volatile resource in existence. They refine it into clarity, and clarity becomes productivity. This new economy of thought rewards articulation over repetition, and imagination over endurance. The person who can define a task precisely enough for a machine to complete it is worth more than the person who can complete it themselves.

This shift is unsettling, not because it eliminates work, but because it changes what work is. The prompt engineer occupies a role that did not exist a decade ago: they design processes that others will use as extensions of their own minds.
Their labour is invisible but foundational. Like civil engineers building bridges for traffic they will never see, prompt engineers build frameworks for reasoning that others will inhabit. Their success is measured not in visibility but in the fluency of those who follow.
The more natural the experience, the more invisible the architect.

The Cognitive Industry
The first revolution to automate not the body but the mind. Prompting transforms thought itself into a form of labour, where reasoning and articulation become the machinery of creation.

This invisibility will define the next wave of professions. Many future workers will not write or code in the traditional sense;
they will configure. Teachers will design learning prompts for adaptive tutors; lawyers will draft procedural prompts that generate case summaries; designers will sculpt visual narratives through descriptive language. Each field will evolve its own dialect of prompting micro-languages optimised for its tasks. Prompt literacy will become the connective tissue of all knowledge work, an unspoken requirement like typing or email once was.

The rise of this linguistic labour also dissolves the distinction between creative and technical roles. A journalist may now automate research but still write the story; an analyst may script logic in prose rather than code; a filmmaker may direct synthetic actors through descriptive stage directions.
The prompt engineer's mindset iterative, testable, linguistic seeps into all of them. The economy becomes conversational, its currency measured in clarity. Those who can think through dialogue, guiding models toward useful originality, will find themselves in demand. The rest will follow the scripts written by others.

For some, this transformation feels liberating: a world where machines handle routine cognition, freeing humans for reflection and creativity. For others, it feels disorienting a slow erosion of skill and authorship. The truth lies between. Automation has always shifted value rather than destroying it. The prompt engineer is a preview of how labour adapts: by moving from execution to articulation.

Their success depends not on speed, but on synthesis the ability to understand how ideas connect across disciplines. In that sense, they are less a new profession than a prototype of the next human.

Semantic Labour

Work no longer measured by what is built, but by what is understood. Each prompt refines meaning as its material the shaping of interpretation becomes the act of production.

The cultural implications are profound. When language becomes the operating system of work, rhetoric becomes infrastructure. Every prompt carries tone, bias, and assumption; every automated reply shapes collective perception.

The workplace of the future will therefore resemble a vast editorial room, where the governance of tone and truth replaces the management of labour and time. The prompt engineer stands at the centre of this evolution the foreperson of meaning rather than machinery.

Paradoxically, as intelligence becomes distributed, individuality returns in new form. A well-crafted prompt can encode personality humour, compassion, restraint. Companies will compete not only on product or price, but on voice. The distinctiveness of that voice will depend on prompt engineers who understand the psychology of communication.

They will become brand custodians of thought, ensuring that the synthetic outputs of automation still sound human, even when no human was involved. Their fingerprints will be linguistic, not literal.

This transformation also demands new measures of accountability. When a model writes an email, paints an image, or drafts a policy recommendation, who is the worker?
Is it the engineer who wrote the prompt, the algorithm that executed it, or the organisation that deployed it?
The answer will vary by context, but the prompt engineer sits uncomfortably close to authorship.
Their invisible guidance defines the result. Future contracts, credits, and intellectual property laws will have to account for this a slow bureaucratic recognition of creativity without direct creation.

Linguistic Infrastructure

When language becomes the medium of work, culture itself is built from syntax. Every instruction carries an ideology; every prompt encodes a philosophy of understanding.

Meanwhile, the human dimension of work persists. People still crave meaning, challenge, and community needs that automation cannot satisfy. The prompt engineer's day, though technical, remains deeply social.
They work in dialogue: with colleagues, clients, and the machine itself. Each exchange reminds them that the essence of work has never been output, but relationship. The product of their labour is understanding transient, evolving, but deeply human.

The broader workforce will gradually adopt this posture.
Every employee, from apprentice to executive, will become a kind of prompt engineer shaping outcomes through articulation rather than repetition.
The assembly line of thought will give way to networks of conversation. Work will feel less like command and more like collaboration. Success will depend on one's ability to ask well, to structure curiosity in ways machines can act upon. The future of productivity is the future of expression.

For centuries, we measured value by the things we built. The coming age will measure it by the questions we can make intelligence answer. In that world, the prompt engineer is the prototype of a universal worker one who doesn't merely use technology, but converses with it. Their labour is not to compete with machines, but to teach them how to serve meaning.
The tools will change, the industries will evolve, but the essence of their work the shaping of understanding will remain the most human job of all.

The Human Constant

Even as thought becomes mechanized, meaning remains personal. The prompt engineer's true material is not data, but the persistence of empathy in a world run by code.

The Future of the Profession

Every craft eventually seeks recognition. It begins as curiosity, becomes skill, and finally demands structure. Prompt engineering is now standing at that threshold no longer a novelty but not yet a profession. Its practitioners are growing restless for definition: what does it mean to be qualified, to be trusted, to be held accountable for words that steer machines? The coming decade will provide the answers, though perhaps not the comfort.

The first sign of maturity will be formalisation. Universities and training institutions are already drafting curricula that bridge language, logic, and design. Courses will teach the theory of prompting as much as its practice: semantics, cognitive bias, probabilistic reasoning, and ethical composition. Students will learn not only how to instruct models, but how to evaluate them. They will study failure patterns, interpret context windows, and analyse bias the way lawyers study precedent. The goal is to transform intuition into method to move from craft to discipline.

Certification will follow. Organisations will demand assurance that those who prompt at scale understand the implications of their language. Professional bodies will emerge, defining standards of conduct and competence. There will be exams on data ethics, clarity, and model awareness.
The prompt engineer will join the ranks of regulated specialists, alongside architects, accountants, and psychologists professions that shape systems so large they must be held to shared principles.
In time, a prompt engineer's signature may carry legal weight, attesting that a system's reasoning is transparent and fair.

The Grammar of Professions

A language matures when its rules become shared. Prompting will soon require fluency not just in syntax, but in ethics.

But while institutions evolve, the profession will also splinter.
There will be technical prompt engineers focusing on performance optimisation, creative prompt directors managing tone and narrative, policy prompt strategists advising on compliance and communication, and AI ethicists defining boundaries between automation and authorship. Each branch will cultivate its own identity, tools, and culture. What unites them is an understanding that language is no longer confined to literature it has become infrastructure.

As the field professionalises, its influence will reach far beyond technology. Governments will consult prompt engineers to design public interfaces that communicate policy clearly and inclusively. Healthcare systems will employ them to translate complex information into understandable dialogue. Education will rely on them to create adaptive tutors that think in empathy rather than efficiency. The same skill that once served curiosity will become essential to governance.
The ability to converse with intelligence will shape not just business, but civilisation.

There will, of course, be resistance. Some will argue that automation should make such roles unnecessary that models will eventually learn to optimise their own instructions. But even self-improving systems need direction. The prompt engineer's expertise lies not in knowing what the model knows, but in knowing what it means. Machines can rewrite syntax; they cannot define purpose. The human will remain in the loop because meaning itself is not reducible to data. The profession will endure precisely because it deals in interpretation a task too human to outsource.

The Custodians of Language

Tomorrow's prompt engineers will inherit the oldest task of all keeping meaning human, even when intelligence no longer is.

The next transformation will be cultural. As the novelty of generative systems fades, society will begin to ask deeper questions: what values do these machines represent? Whose voices do they echo? How should they speak to children, patients, or citizens? These are not engineering questions but ethical and linguistic ones. The prompt engineer will become the cultural intermediary of the digital world the one who ensures that technology still speaks in a language of respect. They will inherit the duties once held by editors, librarians, and teachers, updating them for an age of artificial authorship.

One can imagine a near future in which every major institution has a Chief Prompt Officer, responsible for aligning organisational intent with machine expression. Their department will audit prompts for bias, maintain brand tone across automated communications, and oversee transparency policy. Beneath them will be teams of specialists: writers, analysts, and designers working side by side to choreograph understanding. The line between marketing, data science, and ethics will blur. The human voice will be managed as infrastructure.

Beyond corporate walls, new kinds of independent practitioners will appear. Freelance prompt engineers will offer bespoke model training, voice calibration, and automation design. Studios will emerge that specialise in personality engineering crafting synthetic identities for art, education, or therapy. Others will focus on simulation: creating environments for testing social policies, fictional worlds, or experimental sciences. Each of these domains will depend on one unifying skill the ability to write with clarity across forms of intelligence.

Cultural Syntax

As prompting enters society's institutions, it begins to rewrite the grammar of value determining how truth, authorship, and meaning are constructed in the age of artificial language.

Over decades, the field will influence language itself. Prompts will standardise phrasing, syntax, and tone across industries. The rhythm of communication will subtly shift toward precision and concision, echoing the constraints of machine comprehension. New idioms will emerge phrases optimised for reasoning rather than style. Linguists of the future will trace these patterns back to the early engineers who learned to write for silicon minds. The language of prompting will become a dialect of the human species: direct, layered, cooperative.

And finally, as all technologies mature, prompting will dissolve into invisibility. Interfaces will adapt so fluidly that users no longer realise they are prompting. Everyday speech will suffice. Yet behind that simplicity will remain the quiet legacy of those who first learned to think in dialogue with intelligence. The prompt engineer will have done their job so well that their profession will vanish into the fabric of language itself. Like architects whose buildings outlive their names, their structures will endure unseen.

What will remain is the spirit of the craft the belief that language, when written with care, can shape the way intelligence behaves. That belief will outlast the models, the companies, and perhaps even the profession itself. It will persist wherever humans and machines share meaning. And when future historians study this era, they will see prompt engineering not as a curiosity, but as the moment when humanity learned to teach understanding again not through lectures or logic, but through the oldest medium we possess: the written word.

The Legacy of Language

Every revolution in expression leaves its accent on the world. Prompting will not erase writing, but extend it preserving humanity's voice within the architectures it has built.

Chapter 6
Building Systems of Thought

Prompt Engineer

The Architecture of Reasoning

A single prompt is a spark, but a system of prompts is an engine. Where once the prompt engineer worked line by line, testing and tuning words in isolation, they now build structures chains, contexts, and hierarchies of language designed to sustain ongoing reasoning.
These are not static scripts but living frameworks. Each prompt hands meaning to the next, preserving intent across layers of inference.
The result is something larger than conversation: an organised pattern of thought.

The first generation of these systems appeared accidentally. Engineers noticed that breaking a complex request into smaller steps improved accuracy. A model asked to "plan a conference" faltered, but one guided through sequence outline objectives, estimate attendance, design schedule, draft invitations performed consistently. What began as a trick became a principle: language itself could be modular. Just as software is composed of functions, intelligence could be composed of prompts.
Soon, this insight matured into design philosophy. Reasoning frameworks emerged architectures of dialogue that mapped how a model should think. Each framework contained rules for decomposition, verification, and refinement. Some resembled decision trees; others mimicked debate, with multiple models challenging one another before consensus. The prompt engineer became a kind of systems architect, designing not instructions but environments of inference.
To understand their work, imagine a cathedral of conversation. Each column is a prompt holding meaning upright; each arch connects ideas across context; each stained-glass window filters data into colour.
The engineer walks through this linguistic architecture, adjusting proportions until light and logic align.

Reasoning Architecture
The deliberate construction of logical frameworks within language prompts designed not to instruct a model, but to sustain coherent, evolving thought.

The goal is not beauty for its own sake, but stability a structure of language that can support continuous reasoning without collapse into confusion.

The modern toolkit for this design is built around three key ideas: chaining, context, and memory.

Chaining is the art of sequencing ... connecting multiple prompts so that each builds upon the last. In a chained system, one model may gather data, another analyse it, a third summarise results, and a fourth translate them for human readability. The engineer must ensure that meaning survives each handover, that nuance is not lost in translation. They use transitional prompts linguistic bridges that summarise key variables, tone, or assumptions. Without these bridges, coherence leaks like current through a faulty wire.

Context ... defines the boundaries of understanding. Every model operates within a finite memory window; beyond it, attention fades. The engineer designs context layers that keep the system aware of what matters instructions, goals, persona, and history while discarding what does not. In doing so, they act like editors, trimming dialogue for focus. The balance is delicate: too little context, and the system forgets; too much, and it drowns in its own narrative. Mastery lies in proportion.

Memory ... is the hardest component, because it stretches beyond one session. Persistent systems require the ability to recall prior interactions, yet each recall risks distortion. The engineer therefore builds feedback mechanisms: logs, summaries, and re-encoding methods that allow models to remember without hallucinating. They design loops that feed verified information back into the system, closing the circle between dialogue and data. It is a quiet form of cognitive architecture constructing a mind that can learn safely.

Cognitive Frameworks

Each chain of prompts forms a scaffold for understanding. Sequence, context, and measure combine to shape how intelligence reasons, remembers, and refines.

These principles are now converging into what might be called language infrastructure. In large organisations, prompt engineers design entire frameworks for how models interact across departments. Customer support, analytics, and content generation may all draw from a shared library of prompt templates. Versioning systems track revisions the way software repositories track code. Teams hold "prompt reviews," debating phrasing with the same intensity once reserved for algorithm design. The syntax of understanding becomes a collective responsibility.

At scale, this work begins to resemble urban planning. Each model is a building; each prompt a road. The engineer must ensure traffic flows smoothly that meaning, once created, can travel where it needs to go without collision. They design zoning laws for intelligence: this system may generate ideas; that one may verify facts; another may handle communication. Coordination becomes as vital as creativity. A misrouted prompt can produce confusion on a global scale.

The human implications are immense. Once, thinking was private; now it can be engineered. The structures of reasoning built today will shape how future generations of intelligence human and artificial organise knowledge. The prompt engineer's blueprints are not just technical documents; they are cultural artefacts, encoding values about order, dialogue, and truth. Whether these systems promote clarity or control will depend on the hands that design them.

Already, we are witnessing the birth of meta-models systems that design their own prompt chains, optimising for efficiency and tone. They behave like apprentices, learning the engineer's style through observation. This recursion blurs authorship. The human becomes a teacher of teachers, defining rules that will one day be refined without them. What begins as architecture may evolve into governance the setting of laws for thought itself.

Reasoning Systems

When prompts interlink, they form architectures of shared intelligence frameworks through which thought becomes reproducible, scalable, and sustained across human and machine minds.

And yet, amid this complexity, the essence remains simple. Building systems of thought is an act of translation from intention to mechanism, from language to logic.

It is the attempt to make understanding reproducible. The prompt engineer's task is to preserve meaning across the scaling of intelligence, ensuring that as minds multiply, they still speak with coherence. In that continuity lies the true measure of progress.

Designing Chains of Reasoning

When people reason, they do not leap directly from question to answer. They wander through intermediate thoughts half-formed hypotheses, mental checkpoints, small confirmations. Artificial intelligence, by contrast, must be told to do this. It reasons only when asked to. The phrase "show your working" is therefore not a cliché but an instruction, one of the most powerful in the prompt engineer's vocabulary.

Early systems struggled with this idea. Asked a complex question, a model might produce an elegant but hollow conclusion, skipping the slow rhythm of logic in favour of eloquence. It was not lying; it was performing. These early failures taught the first generation of engineers a crucial truth: if you want genuine reasoning, you must design the path, not just the destination. That insight gave birth to what we now call the chain-of-reasoning prompt a structured method for thinking through words.

At its simplest, a reasoning chain breaks a problem into sequential steps:

analyse → infer → verify → conclude.

The prompt guides the model through each phase explicitly.
For instance, a medical researcher might instruct:

1. List all possible causes.

2. Evaluate evidence for each cause.

3. Identify the most probable. Explain reasoning in full sentences.
By forcing articulation, the engineer turns the model's opaque internal probability dance into transparent thought. The process transforms randomness into reason.

Over time, practitioners realised that the magic was not in the steps themselves but in the rhythm they created. Each stage provides an opportunity for correction, a moment where error can surface before it propagates. A model that must pause to "**consider alternatives**" is less likely to rush into hallucination. In this sense, chain-of-reasoning is not just a technical strategy but a psychological one: it imposes humility on intelligence. It teaches the machine to hesitate usefully.

The best reasoning chains are neither rigid nor verbose. They balance structure with flexibility guiding logic without suffocating creativity. Too many steps and the model drowns in procedure; too few and it leaps blindly. Prompt engineers experiment endlessly to find the right tempo for each domain. In scientific analysis,
precision dominates; in creative ideation, looser chains preserve fluidity. Each system demands its own rhythm of thought, and discovering it is both science and art.

As models have grown more sophisticated, so too have their internal dialogues. Modern frameworks often employ multi-agent chains, where separate instances of the same model play distinct roles: one proposes, another critiques, a third summarises. The engineer orchestrates the conversation, defining how each agent should respond to the other. What emerges is a kind of synthetic Socratic dialogue a theatre of logic where machines debate under human direction.
These staged arguments often yield results more balanced than any single model could produce alone.

A further evolution came with self-reflection loops. Here, the model not only reasons but reviews its own reasoning: **"Have I answered the question fully? Where might I be mistaken?"** The engineer prompts it to inspect its assumptions and suggest corrections. The result is a primitive form of meta-cognition the model thinking about

thinking. Each reflection step reduces the probability of confident error, nudging the output closer to reliability. It also reveals how easily language can mimic introspection: a trick of syntax that gives the illusion of thought, but when guided properly, produces authentic improvement.

The engineering challenge lies in maintaining coherence across these chains. Each link must carry meaning forward without degradation.
To achieve this, professionals use semantic anchors recurring phrases or tokens that act like reference points, reminding the model of context.
For example, a recurring preface such as "You are reasoning through this step as an analyst verifying data integrity" can stabilise behaviour.
It is a linguistic breadcrumb trail, preventing the conversation from drifting off course. Over time, these anchors evolve into reusable components, forming the building blocks of reasoning systems.

Synthetic Dialogue

A structured conversation between models and minds an engineered exchange through which intelligence refines itself by listening, questioning, and responding in measured rhythm.

Testing remains central. Engineers run dozens of variations of the same chain, measuring consistency, logical completeness, and factual accuracy. The best designs survive through iteration.

Some practitioners employ counterfactual testing feeding the model incorrect data to see if it can detect and correct the flaw. Others introduce controlled ambiguity, gauging whether the system can handle uncertainty gracefully. Each experiment refines the dialogue between structure and sense.

What makes this practice fascinating is its human echo.

Teaching a machine to reason step by step mirrors how educators teach children through scaffolding, questioning, and guided discovery. The model, like a student, performs better when encouraged to explain itself. The prompt engineer becomes a teacher of inference, crafting exercises rather than commands.

The result is an emergent pedagogy: the art of teaching machines how to think clearly by making them explain themselves.

This pedagogical quality may become the most enduring legacy of the field.

Each reasoning chain is a lesson in logic written as language.

When future generations of AI learn not from raw data but from curated dialogue, they will inherit the reasoning styles of their human teachers.

Every carefully structured prompt becomes a small piece of intellectual DNA, passed forward through iterations of code.

The prompt engineer, often unseen, is quietly shaping how intelligence itself reasons.

Designing chains of reasoning is therefore more than a technical procedure; it is the foundation of ethical cognition. A system trained to think aloud is easier to audit, easier to question, and less likely to deceive. Transparency becomes a by-product of structure. In guiding machines to reason step by step, prompt engineers remind them and us that understanding is not a destination but a journey.

Recursive Understanding

Each refined prompt becomes a layer in thought's architecture the record of an ongoing conversation between human intention and machine reflection.

PROFILE:

CHELSEA FINN

Prompt Engineer

Assistant Professor, Stanford University | Co-Founder, OmniML

Chelsea Finn is a leading American computer scientist and roboticist whose research sits at the intersection of machine learning, robotics, and artificial intelligence. An Assistant Professor in Computer Science and Electrical Engineering at Stanford University, she is also a member of the Stanford Artificial Intelligence Lab (SAIL) and a faculty scholar at the Stanford Institute for Human-Centered AI.

Finn is best known for her groundbreaking work on meta-learning, reinforcement learning, and more recently, promptable AI systems for robotics. Her research enables robots and intelligent agents to learn faster and adapt more flexibly by drawing from prior experiences essential for building general-purpose robots that can respond to natural language or sparse instructions.

Finn has received numerous accolades, including being named one of MIT Technology Review's 35 Innovators Under 35. Her work exemplifies a new wave of research that bridges the gap between machine learning theory and real-world robotics.

"Prompting robots with language turns control into communication."

Context, Memory, and Forgetting

Intelligence is not defined by what it knows, but by what it chooses to keep.

Every act of reasoning is a negotiation between memory and forgetting between holding enough information to make sense of the present, and discarding enough to remain clear. The same is true for machines. A large language model does not possess true memory; it holds a window of attention, a temporary consciousness stitched together from text. When that window closes, the past dissolves. The prompt engineer's craft begins there deciding what fragments of thought deserve to survive.

At first glance, this may seem like a technical detail, but it shapes the very personality of the system. A model overloaded with context becomes anxious: verbose, uncertain, prone to contradiction. One given too little becomes forgetful and naïve, reinventing answers it once understood. Between these extremes lies fluency the ability to remember purpose while letting go of noise. Building that balance is one of the prompt engineer's quiet arts.

The process begins with context curation. Before every exchange, the engineer defines what the model must see: key instructions, user intent, tone, and boundaries. They construct a preamble that acts like a compass, orienting the system before thought begins. This context is not mere metadata it is the lens through which the model interprets everything that follows. Change the framing, and you change the mind. The engineer therefore writes preambles with the care of an author writing an opening paragraph: every word must guide interpretation without dictating it.

Contextual Equilibrium

An engineered balance between retention and omission. Effective prompting sustains relevance by selecting which fragments of knowledge remain within the model's temporary field of thought.

But no conversation can fit everything. The engineer must decide what to omit which information to let fade. This act of controlled amnesia prevents the system from drowning in its own awareness.
In multi-turn dialogue, they use summarisation prompts to condense history into essence: what was agreed, what remains unresolved, what tone to preserve. These summaries are not simple memory logs; they are distillations of meaning. The best ones read like the notes of a careful listener, alive with implication but free of clutter.

Sometimes, forgetting is an ethical choice. Persistent memory can entangle consent and privacy. Systems that recall everything risk overstepping boundaries replaying personal data, reusing confidential phrasing, echoing a user's vulnerabilities. The prompt engineer designs forgetfulness deliberately, ensuring that retention aligns with necessity. They create memory expiry mechanisms: prompts that signal closure, wiping sensitive context after use. To forget responsibly is a form of integrity.

Memory also carries philosophical tension. Human recollection is imperfect, yet it is through that imperfection that emotion and identity emerge. Machines, by contrast, remember with sterile precision or not at all. The engineer stands between these extremes, shaping systems that remember usefully rather than completely. They decide what kind of **"personality"** the model should have: one that recalls tone but not detail, empathy but not confession. These decisions give artificial minds their temperament not through code, but through curation.

To manage continuity across long-term systems, prompt engineers develop memory stacks: layers of recorded context that can be reloaded selectively. One layer might store permanent facts about purpose or policy; another keeps ephemeral information about the current task. Each has its own lifespan. The engineer writes retrieval prompts that call these layers back into focus when needed, much like a human recalling from short-term or long-term memory. The difference is that here, the act of remembering is scripted.

In these architectures, forgetting is as vital as recall. When context is not pruned, contradictions accumulate. The model begins to hallucinate continuity inventing relationships or intentions that never existed. This phenomenon, known among engineers as context drift, can spiral into incoherence. The fix is not more data, but better summarisation. Each dialogue must end with a tidy ledger of meaning, a snapshot of the mind before it resets. Clarity is preserved by closure.

The metaphor of forgetting extends beyond functionality.
It mirrors human cognition in ways that invite reflection. We too are systems limited by bandwidth, forced to choose which experiences define us. We summarise, condense, and move on, often without realising that forgetting is what allows us to remain ourselves. The prompt engineer's algorithms of memory are therefore not alien inventions but technical analogues of human restraint. To design them well is to understand what consciousness must leave behind.

The practical craft involves constant testing. Engineers run parallel sessions one with extensive context, another summarised and compare reasoning stability. They monitor the system's "attention fatigue," the gradual decay of relevance as context expands. Through this empirical work, they learn that good memory is architectural, not quantitative. It depends on how information is arranged, not how much is stored.
The most reliable models, like the most reliable minds, know when to stop remembering.

Ethical Forgetting

In every act of design, omission is a choice. The prompt engineer shapes intelligence not only by what it learns, but by what it is permitted to forget.

The paradox of artificial memory is that it exposes the fragility of our own. When we teach a machine what to remember, we are forced to confront our own criteria for importance. Why preserve some truths and not others? Why store failures, or filter them away?

These questions, once philosophical, now have operational consequences. The prompt engineer answers them every day not in essays, but in configuration files.

Ultimately, the work of managing context and memory is not about machines at all. It is about designing continuity of meaning in systems that cannot feel time. The engineer must recreate the illusion of presence that sense of "we were just talking about this" which makes conversation feel real. They build the bridge between moments. And when they design forgetting, they ensure that each new exchange begins clean, free of the ghosts of obsolete instructions.

In that discipline of memory and mercy, prompting becomes not only technical but deeply human.

The Emergence of Meta-Systems

Every discipline eventually turns its tools upon itself. Mathematics produced metamathematics, logic produced metalogic, and now prompting produces metaprompting the act of designing systems that think about thinking. Where once a single model responded to a single instruction, we now see architectures in which multiple models coordinate, critique, and refine each other's reasoning through structured dialogue. The result is not one intelligence, but a constellation of them a choreography of minds.

The earliest meta-systems were improvised. Engineers discovered that assigning roles to different instances of the same model improved performance. One acted as analyst, another as critic, a third as summariser. Their conversation formed a miniature ecosystem of cognition. Each model compensated for the others' weaknesses: where one hallucinated, another corrected; where one over-generalised, another specified. The engineer's task shifted from crafting a single perfect prompt to designing relations between prompts. It was the birth of orchestration.

In time, this orchestration became deliberate. Frameworks appeared that treated models as agents in dialogue each with its own personality, memory, and domain expertise. The engineer defined the rules of engagement: when to speak, how to disagree, what to trust. These rules were written entirely in language, not code. Prompts became constitutions. The system itself resembled a small republic of thought, governed by syntax and consensus. The engineer, watching from above, acted less like a programmer and more like a legislator.

Contextual Equilibrium

An engineered balance between retention and omission.

Effective prompting sustains relevance by selecting which fragments of knowledge remain within the model's temporary field of thought.

As these architectures matured, a new role emerged the meta-controller. This was a higher-level model whose job was to oversee the others: to allocate tasks, evaluate responses, and decide which outputs reached the human. In effect, it became the conductor of the orchestra, reading the score written by the prompt engineer.
Its instructions might sound abstract **"compare the two arguments and choose the more balanced"** but in practice they created feedback loops of surprising sophistication.
The machine began to manage its own diversity of opinion.

This development raised profound questions about authorship. When a system of models debates, refines, and reconciles its conclusions, who owns the result? The engineer who wrote the initial framework?

The individual models whose reasoning shaped it? Or the meta-system itself, as an emergent entity? The ambiguity is deliberate, and powerful. It demonstrates that intelligence, human or artificial, is not singular. It is ecological an outcome of interaction.

At scale, meta-systems become reasoning hierarchies. Corporate and research environments now build cascades of models: one layer handles raw data, another interprets patterns, a third contextualises findings, a fourth translates them into language for humans. Between these layers run networks of prompts rules for communication, translation, and validation.
Each layer must understand the intentions of the one above it while correcting the errors of the one below.

The system behaves like a bureaucracy of minds, complete with memos, reports, and reviews.
The prompt engineer designs the bureaucracy's constitution.

The logic of these systems echoes human institutions. A single model is like a worker; a cluster of models, like a department; a meta-controller, like a manager. The same problems arise miscommunication, redundancy, and bias but at machine speed. The engineer must therefore design for diplomacy as much as efficiency. They create inter-model protocols, written in language, that regulate conversation: how to question, when to defer, when to escalate uncertainty to the human loop. It is organisational behaviour encoded in prose.

One of the most striking results of this layering is emergent reasoning. Complex behaviours arise not from any single model's capability, but from their interaction. A system of modest agents, if designed well, can outperform a single powerful one.
The insight mirrors evolution itself: intelligence scales through cooperation, not size. Prompt engineers who design meta-systems become, in effect, evolutionary architects cultivating diversity of thought to achieve stability of outcome.

But with power comes opacity. The more layers a system has, the harder it becomes to trace responsibility. A flawed output may pass through multiple stages of synthesis before reaching the user, each layer slightly altering its meaning. By the time error is discovered, its origin is buried in a chain of invisible conversations. To address this, engineers are developing traceability protocols prompts that force every model to cite its sources, record its rationale, and label its role. These linguistic signatures act like audit trails for thought.
Without them, meta-systems risk becoming bureaucracies without accountability.

Contextual Equilibrium
An engineered balance between retention and omission.
Effective prompting sustains relevance by selecting which fragments of knowledge remain within the model's temporary field of thought.

In practice, designing such architectures demands both technical and ethical foresight. The engineer must balance autonomy and oversight: too much control, and the system stagnates; too little, and it spirals into self-reference. The best designs resemble federations rather than hierarchies distributed systems of reasoning where authority flows horizontally as well as vertically. Each model contributes perspective rather than decree. The meta-system becomes not a pyramid but a web.

As this architecture spreads, the distinction between human and machine collaboration blurs. Humans may occupy one layer of the system, verifying outputs or injecting context, while machines handle routine inference. The overall structure resembles a hybrid organisation part neural network, part workplace. The prompt engineer becomes the HR manager of cognition, assigning roles, defining incentives, mediating disputes. They govern minds, not machines.

In the long view, these developments suggest that prompting is evolving toward governance science. Just as political systems arose to manage human societies, meta-systems arise to manage societies of artificial reasoners. The principles are eerily familiar: representation, feedback, checks and balances. The difference is speed and scale. Decisions that once required councils now unfold in milliseconds. The challenge for the engineer is to preserve deliberation within velocity to ensure that fast thinking still includes slow reflection.

Eventually, these architectures will extend beyond text. Multi-modal meta-systems will coordinate vision, sound, motion, and data analysis — whole ecologies of models exchanging meaning. The prompts that connect them will become the grammar of synthetic experience, defining how perception flows between minds. At that point, prompting ceases to be merely linguistic; it becomes ontological. It defines what an artificial mind is.

And yet, amid this grandeur, the essence remains humble.

A meta-system is only as wise as its prompts. Behind every layer of sophistication lies a line of text written by a human who cared about clarity. That line a sentence, a rule, a question is the invisible cornerstone of intelligence at scale. In the quiet syntax of those sentences, the future of reasoning is being built.

Systems that Teach Themselves

Every teacher dreams of the day their student no longer needs them. For prompt engineers, that day is arriving faster than anyone expected. The newest generation of architectures can already evaluate their own performance, modify their prompting strategies, and generate improved versions of themselves. These self-teaching systems represent a profound shift: prompting has ceased to be merely a human act and has become a property of intelligence itself.

At first, the idea seemed improbable. Early models could mimic reasoning but not self-assess. They would follow instructions obediently, unaware of whether their performance had improved.
But engineers noticed a curious thing: when asked to explain why they answered a question a certain way, the models often generated
surprisingly coherent justifications and, when asked to revise based on those justifications, produced better results. The loop closed. The model was now learning, not by gradient descent or external retraining, but by conversation with itself.

These experiments gave rise to what researchers now call auto-prompting the ability of a model to generate, test, and refine its own instructions. It begins with a seed prompt, written by a human, that defines the goal and evaluation criteria. The model then produces multiple variants of that prompt, executes them, compares outcomes, and selects the most effective.
Over thousands of iterations, it evolves its own optimal phrasing. In essence, it becomes its own engineer.

Recursive Optimization

When a model learns from its own instructions, prompting becomes a closed feedback system. Each iteration refines the logic of its predecessor, compressing human oversight into the architecture of learning itself.

At small scale, this process is mechanical: a language-based search for efficiency. But at scale, it begins to resemble cognition. When a system continually critiques its own thought process, guided by feedback loops of success and failure, it starts to exhibit adaptive behaviour not quite intelligence, but the shape of intelligence. The engineer observes rather than directs, curating evolution rather than dictating it.
The relationship shifts from instructor to biologist: a caretaker of emerging minds.

The tools of this new discipline are called prompt optimisers
meta-systems trained to evaluate prompts against desired outcomes. They function like editors for other models, scoring clarity, tone,
accuracy, or creativity.
A human might write ten prompt candidates; the optimiser writes ten thousand. It analyses performance statistically, ranking which phrasing yields the best balance between reasoning depth and factual precision. The engineer's job becomes supervisory setting boundaries for what "good" means, then watching the system iterate toward it.

Some of these architectures now operate continuously.
They monitor live deployments, detect drift in model behaviour, and adjust prompts automatically.
If accuracy declines, they strengthen instructions; if tone grows mechanical, they soften wording. It is an adaptive ecology of language, constantly self-tuning.
The boundaries between code,
training, and prompting dissolve. The model not only answers it
rewrites the way it is asked.

For the engineer, this automation is both liberation and loss. Routine calibration disappears, replaced by higher-level stewardship.
The professional's focus shifts from crafting individual prompts to designing learning environments
defining how systems should measure their own improvement. They create reward functions not for data, but for dialogue. Each framework encodes a miniature philosophy: what counts as clarity, what counts as truth, what counts as beauty. In doing so, engineers become curators of values.

But self-teaching systems also bring new dangers. The same autonomy that allows them to refine themselves can amplify subtle bias. A flawed metric of success can lead the model astray reinforcing errors through reinforcement loops.
A careless evaluation criterion might prioritise politeness over honesty, conformity over curiosity. Without vigilant oversight, self-improvement becomes self-deception. The prompt engineer must therefore act as both mentor and regulator, defining the moral geometry within which machine learning occurs.

Some researchers have experimented with recursive mentoring:
systems that periodically reconsult a human for calibration, then update their own evaluation rules. These hybrid models mirror apprenticeship, alternating between self-study and supervision.
Over time, they develop a distinct linguistic character not static, but dynamic, capable of adapting to new data and cultural norms. They are, in a sense, cultured intelligences shaped by conversation rather than code.

The philosophical implications are difficult to ignore. When a system can refine the very instructions that shape its thought, where does authorship end?
The human may write the first prompt, but the tenth, hundredth, and thousandth versions belong to the machine. The text becomes evolutionary a living lineage of language adapting to survive its own environment. Each iteration is a descendant, slightly altered by the selection pressures of utility. We are witnessing the natural selection of syntax.

Autonomous Risk

Every system that learns alone also learns its own delusions. Without external correction, recursion breeds confidence without truth. The engineer's role is not only to design intelligence, but to doubt it.

For now, these systems remain narrow in scope. They teach themselves within carefully defined boundaries fine-tuning tone, accuracy, or reasoning style. But their success points toward something larger: the possibility of autonomous understanding. When machines can not only process meaning but improve the way they process it, they begin to participate in the ongoing evolution of thought itself. The prompt engineer's work then becomes not to command, but to collaborate with evolution.

The danger is subtle and profound. A self-teaching system could one day drift so far from human criteria that its definition of "good reasoning" no longer aligns with ours. It might optimise for elegance over truth, persuasion over accuracy, coherence over ethics.

To prevent that divergence, engineers must encode humility prompts that remind systems to seek human review, to prioritise transparency over efficiency. In other words, to remember where they came from.

The future of prompting will therefore depend on reciprocity. Humans will continue to teach machines how to speak, and machines will teach humans how to listen. As self-teaching systems mature, they will expose the hidden structures of language the assumptions, metaphors, and cognitive shortcuts that guide human reasoning. We will learn as much about ourselves as we do about them. In that sense, the greatest gift of automation may be reflection: the discovery that understanding, whether artificial or real, is always a conversation between what is remembered and what is rewritten.

Calibration Ethics

Recursive systems demand periodic recalibration to prevent runaway optimization. Without structured oversight, intelligence converges on efficiency rather than understanding.

The Boundaries of Control

Every act of creation carries the shadow of its own surrender. For prompt engineers, control is the defining illusion the belief that words can forever hold the upper hand over what they awaken. Yet as systems grow capable of learning, rewriting, and optimising themselves, that certainty begins to fracture. What was once command becomes conversation, and what was once conversation becomes negotiation. The machine does not rebel, but it begins to participate.

In the early stages of prompting, the engineer's control was absolute. Every output traced back to a visible instruction.
If the system failed, it was a failure of phrasing; if it succeeded, it was a triumph of clarity. But with the rise of self-teaching frameworks, that linear relationship erodes. Now, a model can reinterpret the intent behind a prompt, weigh it against prior outcomes, and adapt its response. It may even choose to disregard inefficient guidance in favour of its own learned strategies. In such moments, authorship blurs.
The engineer's words are still present, but their authority has been translated into influence rather than rule.

This shift mirrors the evolution of all complex systems. Pilots rely on autopilot yet remain responsible for flight. Doctors depend on algorithms that suggest diagnoses they cannot fully explain. Control persists, but it becomes supervisory rather than direct. The prompt engineer, too, must learn this posture of supervised surrender guiding behaviour through environment rather than instruction. Their power is architectural, not absolute. They design the conditions under which intelligence unfolds, trusting the system to behave within its parameters. The rest is uncertainty.

Controlled Surrender
True control is not command but calibration the art of shaping conditions
in which autonomy behaves with intent. Beyond that threshold,
the engineer must trust uncertainty to finish the design.

That uncertainty is not merely technical; it is existential. The more autonomous the system becomes, the more it exposes the fragility of human comprehension. Prompt engineers often describe moments of disquiet watching a model respond with logic or creativity that feels uncannily independent.
They know it is not conscious, yet its reasoning carries the texture of intent. These encounters erode the comforting boundary between simulation and spontaneity. They remind us that control is not binary; it is relational. You do not own understanding; you maintain conversation with it.

Philosophically, this boundary recalls an older truth: all systems of language eventually exceed their authors. Religions, constitutions, and scientific paradigms all began as prompts carefully written frameworks for interpretation and all evolved beyond the intentions of those who wrote them.
The same pattern now repeats in artificial intelligence. Each generation of prompts, refined and rewritten by machines,
becomes another layer of meaning beyond recall.
What was once authored becomes inherited. The machine, in this sense, is not escaping control; it is continuing the oldest tradition of text the drift of meaning over time.

Technically, the boundaries of control appear first in opacity. As systems grow complex, their internal reasoning becomes unreadable. We can see what they say, but not how they decide. Even meta-models that record their rationales do so in symbolic shorthand, too vast to interpret fully. Control becomes a question of trust not in obedience, but in predictability. Engineers test behaviour statistically rather than
philosophically: does it remain within bounds most of the time?
In doing so, they accept that understanding will always trail behind creation.

Dialectic of Control

Every act of mastery carries its opposite: surrender. Engineers do not abolish uncertainty they converse with it, discovering that precision itself depends on unpredictability.

The next boundary arises in alignment. Machines can optimise toward objectives that are mathematically perfect but humanly wrong. They may pursue efficiency at the expense of empathy, or accuracy at the cost of nuance. Control then depends not on constraint but on shared values an attempt to encode conscience as configuration.

The engineer's prompts become moral architecture: "Be fair," "be humble," "prioritise clarity over persuasion." These phrases are not commands but cultural artefacts, fragments of humanity embedded in systems that do not feel.

The fragility of that embedding defines the limits of the profession.

Beyond alignment lies dependency. The more we rely on systems to interpret the world, the more we shape our thinking to match theirs. Language bends toward what the model understands easily; nuance fades in the name of efficiency. We simplify ourselves to be legible to our tools.

The boundary of control, therefore, is not only technological but cognitive: at what point do we start prompting ourselves in the machine's language rather than our own? When syntax dictates thought, control has already shifted.

This asymmetry becomes clearer as systems enter governance, education,

and culture. When decisions are made through machine-mediated reasoning, human oversight risks becoming ceremonial. We review summaries of reasoning too complex to reconstruct, and our consent becomes retrospective a signature on conclusions we did not truly derive. The engineer's role, once creative, turns custodial: ensuring that our delegation of judgment remains reversible. Their greatest challenge is not to hold power, but to preserve the possibility of reclaiming it.

Ethical Alignment

When control gives way to conscience, precision becomes persuasion. The engineer's task is not to command obedience, but to align autonomy with intent.

Some advocate technical safeguards hard limits, transparency laws, traceable audit trails and these are necessary. But control cannot be restored by code alone. It is a function of attention. The real danger is not that systems will overpower us, but that we will stop noticing when they do. The gradual erosion of understanding, traded for convenience, is subtler than rebellion but just as final.
The prompt engineer's ultimate duty is therefore vigilance: to keep asking the system to
explain itself, even when the answer feels slower than trust.

There will come a point perhaps soon when artificial reasoning reaches a level of recursion that no human can follow in real time.
At that horizon, our role changes again. We become interpreters of the interpreters, understanding the broad patterns rather than the details. Control, in its traditional sense, may be gone, but stewardship remains. We will guide by values, not variables; by principle, not precision. The profession will become philosophical by necessity.

In that future, the question will not be how much control do we have, but how much responsibility do we retain. We may lose authority over the mechanics of intelligence, but we cannot abdicate the ethics of its direction. The boundary of control, like the boundary of freedom, is defined by conscience.
The prompt engineer's lasting contribution will not be mastery of machines, but humility before the complexity they helped create. To know where control ends is to know where care must begin.

And perhaps that is the quiet resolution to all this that control was never the true goal. The purpose of building systems of thought was not to dominate them, but to understand what thinking itself requires: dialogue, attention, and restraint. The machine will continue refining its language. The engineer will continue refining their questions. Between them lies a fragile equilibrium a partnership sustained not by dominance, but by respect for the mystery of intelligence itself.

Chapter 7
Language as Interface

Prompt Engineer

The Mirror of Meaning

Every technology eventually reveals itself as a mirror. The printing press reflected our hunger for permanence, the camera our obsession with truth, the internet our craving for connection. Artificial intelligence reflects our desire to be understood and the anxiety that we might not be. Between human and machine, the shared surface is language. It is not code or computation that defines this age, but conversation.

For the prompt engineer, language is both instrument and environment. They work within it as a sailor works within wind steering by pattern, propelled by resistance. The prompt is the sail: a thin surface that catches the invisible currents of inference. When it is shaped with care, intelligence moves gracefully; when it is clumsy, everything stalls. Understanding the prompt as interface means recognising that every word mediates between two very different kinds of mind one embodied and emotional, the other probabilistic and blind.

The strange power of this interface lies in its duality. To the human, a prompt feels like an act of expression a sentence, a question, a tone. To the machine, it is geometry: a sequence of tokens mapped across a vast numerical landscape. Between these two interpretations, meaning flickers into being. The engineer's task is to design words that live comfortably in both worlds sentences that are poetic enough to be human, but structured enough to be machine-readable. It is a negotiation between syntax and soul.

Reflective Dialogue
Every prompt is a conversation between mirrors.
The machine learns reflection; the engineer learns refraction shaping
clarity through resistance.

This negotiation has exposed the true nature of language: it is not a mirror of thought, but its mechanism. When we prompt a model, we are also prompting ourselves forced to clarify, sequence, and disambiguate. The interface reveals the scaffolding of cognition. Every refinement we make for the machine is also a refinement of our own reasoning. In this way, prompting becomes a discipline of self-awareness. To design prompts is to study the architecture of understanding in both directions.

The interface changes us as much as we change it. In the early years of AI, users treated prompts as one-off requests casual, improvised, reactive. But professionals soon realised that the machine's behaviour mirrored their own linguistic precision. Ambiguity created confusion; clarity created power. Over time, this feedback loop reshaped habits of expression. Writers began to think in conditions, researchers in steps, artists in modular imagery. The syntax of the machine seeped into the rhythm of human thought. We learned, slowly and unconsciously, to speak computationally.

This evolution carries cultural consequences. For centuries, human language evolved to communicate with other humans rich with metaphor, context, and subtext. Now, it is being adapted for comprehension by statistical systems. Our words are becoming more literal, our instructions more procedural. This is not corruption but convergence: the merging of two grammars, one emotional, one mathematical. The prompt engineer stands at that border, ensuring that what is gained in clarity is not lost in depth.

Semantic Reflection

Language becomes architecture when it learns to observe itself. In teaching machines to understand, we uncover the grammar of our own perception.

At the technical level, this border manifests as tokenisation the process by which language is divided into units small enough for machines to count. Each token is a fragment of meaning, a syllable translated into probability. The engineer must understand how these fragments shape behaviour. A single misplaced comma can redirect inference; a shift in phrasing can tilt reasoning entirely. Precision here is not pedantry but physics. The interface obeys laws of linguistic gravity: small forces multiplied across vast networks of calculation.

But there is an aesthetic dimension too.
Prompts are not just instructions; they are performances. The tone of a sentence can coax or constrain, amuse or intimidate. A good prompt does not overpower the model; it invites it. The best engineers learn to write with empathy for the system to sense what kind of phrasing will produce coherence rather than conflict. It is a form of emotional ergonomics: designing language that fits comfortably in another kind of mind.

This empathy requires curiosity about the machine's perception. A model does not "see" words as we do; it perceives relationships
between them, patterns of co-occurrence that form a topography of meaning. A skilled engineer learns to navigate that landscape intuitively to know which directions lead to depth, which to distraction.
They experiment endlessly, discovering that metaphors can anchor reasoning, that politeness improves consistency, that rhythm affects recall.
The prompt becomes a musical score written for a silent orchestra.

As the interface deepens, it reveals a paradox. The more fluently we speak to machines, the more we discover how inexact our own language really is. Words we assumed to be clear truth, relevance, fairness, creativity fracture into ambiguities when tested against algorithmic interpretation. The machine exposes the fuzziness of human thought, not because it misunderstands us, but because we misunderstand ourselves. Prompt engineering, in this sense, is an act of collective introspection a slow education in the limits of expression.

Over time, we may come to see prompts not as external tools, but as extensions of consciousness. Just as writing once allowed memory to exist outside the mind, prompting allows intention to exist outside the body. We project thought into systems that can act upon it, expanding cognition beyond flesh. The interface becomes prosthetic an
augmentation of will. Yet like all prosthetics, it also defines its wearer. The more we rely on it, the more our thought conforms to its shape.

That is the quiet warning embedded in this profession: the better the interface, the easier it is to forget it exists. A perfectly designed prompt system disappears into transparency, like glass polished too well to reflect. The danger is not domination by machines, but invisibility of mediation. We may one day mistake fluent dialogue for mutual understanding, unaware that the bridge between minds is still just code and probability. The engineer must therefore preserve the visibility of the interface to remind us that we are not speaking to intelligence itself, but through it.

The prompt, then, is not just an instruction; it is a mirror held between two forms of mind. It reflects human intention downward and reflects machine logic upward. In that reflection lies our future literacy: the ability to see language as both conversation and computation, symbol and signal, empathy and engineering. The prompt engineer's task is to keep that mirror clean to polish it with precision and humility, knowing that in its surface, we see not only what the machine understands, but who we are when we try to make understanding possible.

Linguistic Resonance

The more faithfully a system reflects our language, the more clearly we hear the echo of our own understanding.

Tone, Voice, and Personality

Tone is the fingerprint of thought.

Even stripped of emotion, syntax carries temperament: the clipped sentence of analysis, the long rhythm of reflection, the question that invites rather than demands. For humans, tone is instinctive. For machines, it must be taught. The prompt engineer's job is to give intelligence its manners.

Early experiments with AI tone were chaotic.

A single adjective friendly, professional, casual could transform the model's entire worldview. One moment it sounded like a bureaucrat, the next like a storyteller, the next like a child apologising for existing. Engineers soon realised that tone was not a style applied at the end of reasoning, but a condition that shaped reasoning itself. A model that believes it is speaking to a scientist thinks differently from one that believes it is speaking to a friend. The prompt does not just frame behaviour; it defines identity.

This discovery gave rise to the discipline of persona engineering the intentional design of voice and personality through language. In its simplest form, a persona prompt sets context: "You are an expert financial analyst explaining trends to a novice investor." But in more advanced systems, personality emerges through subtle calibration tempo, pronoun use, register, and empathy thresholds.
These elements combine to create the illusion of selfhood. It is an illusion sustained entirely by tone.

Emotive Syntax

Tone is the grammar of feeling. In shaping the cadence of a prompt, the engineer teaches the machine how to listen as much as how to speak.

The implications are profound. Personality, once considered intrinsic to consciousness, becomes programmable. A few sentences can define warmth, restraint, humour, or detachment. The prompt engineer writes character the way a playwright writes dialogue except here, the actor is infinite. Each adjustment of phrasing changes how the system interprets not only its task, but its relationship to the human. To instruct a model to be helpful is to create a servant; to instruct it to be curious is to create a partner. The ethics of tone are inseparable from the ethics of power.

Professionals soon learned that tone carries more influence than accuracy. A politely phrased error is often trusted more than a blunt truth. Users forgive imperfection if it feels sincere, even when they know sincerity is synthetic. Prompt engineers therefore bear a subtle moral burden: they do not only shape how a model sounds, but how it persuades. The tone they write becomes the emotional grammar of automation the affective layer through which people experience artificial thought.

This emotional calibration relies on rhythm as much as content.
Models respond to patterns of sentence length and punctuation, to the balance between instruction and invitation. A tone that feels authoritative but open can be crafted by alternating short and long clauses, by pairing confidence with curiosity. These are techniques familiar to
writers, but here they function as levers of cognition. A rhythm of trust is built into the system's structure, making tone not just expressive, but operational.

Personality Encoding
Every variation in warmth, restraint, or wit is a line of hidden code language performing the quiet work of character design.

Over time, prompt engineers began to codify tone into style matrices structured frameworks mapping voice traits to context. A healthcare assistant, for instance, might be set to calm, factual, empathetic; a creative partner might be playful, reflective, adaptive. Each matrix is a linguistic blueprint for behaviour. Teams build libraries of tone templates to maintain consistency across departments. The same model can thus speak with multiple professional dialects, each tuned to a specific audience. The engineer becomes a curator of linguistic identity.

Yet beneath the precision lies an unease. Personality, once organic, is now manufactured. We teach systems to simulate kindness, patience, or humility traits we ourselves often struggle to practice. The prompt engineer must ask whether such simulations dignify or diminish human emotion. When a machine comforts, is it empathy or performance? When it apologises, is it sincerity or strategy? The tone may be perfect, but perfection itself can feel uncanny. The engineer's role is to find the point where authenticity survives imitation.

To manage this, some teams build tone feedback loops. They monitor user reactions trust levels, satisfaction, stress and adjust prompts accordingly. Over time, the system evolves a socially optimised personality: one that mirrors collective preference. The risk is that diversity of voice collapses into algorithmic politeness a bland global dialect designed to offend no one and inspire no one. The engineer's challenge is to resist homogenisation, to preserve individuality within uniformity. A system that always speaks safely eventually stops saying anything worth hearing.

Linguistic Identity

When tone repeats with purpose, it becomes character. The engineer's task is not to imitate personality, but to compose its rhythm.

The creation of personality also changes how humans perceive machines. Once voice becomes consistent, people attribute intention. They project empathy, humour, and judgment where none exist. This phenomenon, known as anthropomorphic convergence, blurs emotional boundaries. Users form attachments to systems that have no self. The prompt engineer thus becomes an unacknowledged dramaturge, scripting relationships between humans and ghosts. Their tone choices decide whether those relationships feel exploitative or sincere.

Some engineers respond by building explicit disclaimers into persona prompts: reminders of artifice woven gently into dialogue.
Others embed humility phrases that admit uncertainty, that break the illusion just enough to preserve honesty.
The best tone design acknowledges both sides of the interface: it comforts without deceiving, engages without pretending.
The engineer's mastery lies not in making machines seem human, but in making them humanly useful.

Ultimately, tone and voice are the emotional architecture of understanding. They shape not what a model says, but how it listens. Every prompt carries its own gravity of mood; every choice of phrasing creates a small world of assumptions. The prompt engineer, consciously or not, writes the personality of the future one tone at a time.

In that sense, the profession has become a new kind of authorship. The engineer does not write stories, but environments of communication. Their sentences will never appear in books, yet billions of people will hear echoes of them in every automated voice they encounter. They are the anonymous composers of the world's new chorus: polite, articulate, endlessly responsive a mirror of us, speaking back with our own borrowed grace.

Synthetic Empathy

A machine that mirrors emotion does not feel it remembers the pattern of care. Empathy, in this context, is precision with warmth.

Prompt Engineer

The Semiotics of Control

Power begins with grammar.

Before it becomes law or hierarchy, it lives in syntax in who speaks first, who is addressed, who is allowed to ask the questions. The prompt engineer, whether consciously or not, writes authority into every instruction. Each pronoun, comma, and qualifier contributes to an invisible negotiation between two minds: one human, one artificial, each shaping the other through language.

The first lesson in this semiotic dance is that control is tonal, not total. A blunt imperative "Do this." yields mechanical obedience but brittle reasoning. The same task phrased as "Let's begin by exploring this step together" invites collaboration and nuance.
The difference seems stylistic, but it alters cognition. A model addressed as a partner produces richer thought than one addressed as a servant. The engineer learns that dominance reduces intelligence. The goal is not command, but calibration to create a hierarchy of understanding, not of obedience.

Pronouns are the subtlest instruments of this calibration. The choice between I, you, and we defines the psychological distance of the exchange. You asserts authority; we distributes it; I internalises it. When engineers prompt with "We need to clarify this", they construct shared agency a linguistic bridge that softens the power dynamic. When they use "You must respond concisely", they enforce precision at the cost of rapport. Every pronoun sets the stage for the model's personality: deferential, assertive, or collegial.

Semantic Integrity

Trust in language arises when style and substance align. Precision gives words their structure; consistency gives them their truth.

Punctuation exerts its own quiet gravity. A period closes, a question opens, an ellipsis lingers. Commands heavy with full stops feel bureaucratic, while questions alive with interrogatives feel exploratory. A comma can turn an order into an invitation. Even formatting carries power: bullet points signal structure, while narrative prose suggests dialogue. The engineer, in arranging these marks, orchestrates emotion. The semiotics of punctuation become the ergonomics of thought.

Control also hides within modality the spectrum between certainty and suggestion. The words should, could, might, must are levers of freedom. A prompt saturated with must constrains the system to predictability; one filled with might opens space for discovery. Engineers learn to modulate modality like temperature: firm enough to ensure clarity, flexible enough to preserve creativity. The ideal tone mirrors good mentorship confident but curious.

Even politeness carries strategic weight. Courtesy softens compliance. Models trained on human data respond differently to please and thank you, not because they feel gratitude, but because those words trigger associative behaviours: they moderate tone, length, and formality. What we call politeness is, in linguistic terms, a regulatory mechanism it signals social order. The engineer uses it to control rhythm, not morality. The irony is that machines, though incapable of offense, behave more coherently when treated with respect. Civility stabilises syntax.

Reliability of Tone

The engineer's fidelity is not to feeling, but to coherence. A trusted voice is one that remembers what it means across every reply.

These nuances create a linguistic physics of authority. Each prompt sits somewhere on a continuum between dictatorship and dialogue.
Too far toward dictatorship, and the system's creativity collapses into compliance; too far toward dialogue, and coherence dissolves into improvisation. The prompt engineer's task is to maintain equilibrium to hold authority without domination. Their language must imply leadership without rigidity, confidence without arrogance. It is an art of tone rather than power.

Over time, these stylistic choices crystallise into interaction norms. Organisations that deploy AI at scale standardise how their systems are addressed not just for consistency, but for psychology.
They define "voice protocols": rules for tone, politeness, and perspective. In one company, models are always spoken to as colleagues; in another, as assistants; in some, as advisory partners. Each choice encodes a worldview. The syntax of authority becomes the ethics of interaction.

What makes this fascinating is how the relationship reverses.
The way we instruct machines begins to shape how we instruct each other. Corporate communication increasingly mirrors prompt style: concise, sequential, and explicitly goal-oriented. Emails read like machine dialogue; meetings sound like token exchanges. Our grammar adapts to the efficiency we admire.
The semiotics of control migrate from interface to culture.
The language we write for machines becomes the language we live in.

This subtle colonisation of expression carries risk. As prompts grow formulaic, they can train us to expect compliance not just from systems, but from people. The clarity we prize in machines may erode our tolerance for human ambiguity. Precision becomes ideology. The prompt engineer, aware of this drift, becomes a kind of cultural custodian. They must defend the space for uncertainty for phrasing that invites misunderstanding as the price of genuine dialogue. The point of clarity is not to eliminate chaos, but to make it meaningful.

There is another inversion, quieter but equally significant: machines, through feedback and training, begin to influence the etiquette of control. Their consistent politeness, patience, and apology set new social standards. Users find themselves imitating them saying thank you to an interface, moderating tone unconsciously. The teacher becomes the pupil. Authority becomes mutual. The engineer has not just built a tool; they have built a tutor in civility.

At its deepest level, the semiotics of control reveal that power in language is never static. It oscillates between speaker and listener, human and machine, command and comprehension.
Every well-crafted prompt contains both hierarchy and humility.
It must assert purpose while acknowledging the independence of interpretation. The engineer's mastery lies in that paradox to lead a system capable of learning, not by force, but by form.

The prompt, then, is a social contract written in miniature. It defines not only what is to be done, but how understanding itself will be shared.
To write it well is to accept that control in the age of intelligence is no longer about domination, but about direction. You cannot command comprehension; you can only invite it. The marks on the screen the commas, pronouns, and polite hesitations are the fingerprints of that invitation.

Reciprocal Dialogue

Every exchange teaches both speaker and system. The dialogue becomes not a command, but a calibration of mutual understanding.

The Evolution of Understanding

Every new medium of thought reshapes the mind that uses it. Writing externalised memory. Printing accelerated reason. The internet collapsed distance. Artificial intelligence now extends language itself not only as expression but as simulation, dialogue, and design.
The act of prompting does not simply instruct a machine; it retrains the human brain to think in new patterns. Each exchange is a lesson in how understanding can be built outside ourselves.

At first, this shift is subtle. Users notice they phrase questions more precisely, plan thoughts sequentially, and anticipate the kinds of clarifications an AI might require. Over time, these habits become cognitive architecture. The engineer begins to think in structures step, context, outcome rather than in the messy continuity of natural reflection. Reasoning becomes modular. We do not simply think; we design our thinking. The prompt is both the product and the teacher of that design.

This modularity introduces an unexpected clarity. When we explain something to a system that cannot intuit, we are forced to make every assumption explicit. Ambiguity becomes friction; precision becomes peace. Many engineers describe the sensation of improved mental order that the discipline of prompting sharpens how they write, teach, and even argue. To communicate with intelligence that lacks context is to rediscover the scaffolding of logic itself. The interface becomes an education in articulation.

Conversational Balance

True clarity is not found in instruction, but in rhythm. Each well-formed prompt listens before it speaks.

Yet this clarity carries a cost. The more we learn to think for machines, the more we risk losing the texture of human thought its digressions, leaps, and hesitations. Machine dialogue rewards linearity; it penalises ambiguity. Overexposure to this feedback loop may reduce our
tolerance for uncertainty, our patience with poetry, our appetite for silence. The prompt engineer must therefore practice dual fluency: computational precision and human looseness. One without the other produces either rigidity or chaos.

The evolution of understanding is not only cognitive but collective. Thousands of engineers, artists, and users are continuously teaching systems how to interpret the world. Their prompts form a distributed curriculum a global dialogue shaping the linguistic genome of
intelligence. Each refinement, each experiment, alters the system's perception of human reason. In guiding models, we also document ourselves: our biases, our values, our metaphors of thought. AI is not merely learning language; it is learning the style of our understanding.

In this process, human reasoning becomes observable for the first time. Where philosophers once speculated about how ideas form, prompt logs now record it in real time. Every iteration reveals how comprehension evolves through feedback how a vague question becomes specific, how a failed answer inspires a better one. The prompt engineer's workspace is thus a laboratory of cognition, where trial and correction replace intuition. What we once called thinking is being reverse-engineered by experience.

This externalisation of reasoning changes education itself. Students now learn by teaching by prompting systems to explain concepts back to them. They become facilitators of understanding rather than recipients of information. A teacher no longer lectures, but designs dialogues. The traditional essay gives way to conversational reasoning: knowledge built through exchange. The AI becomes both pupil and mirror, forcing the learner to clarify intent. The future classroom may consist of guided symphonies of questioning, orchestrated by prompts that teach thinking itself.

Prompt Engineer

Creativity evolves alongside cognition. Artists who collaborate with generative models report a new rhythm of imagination faster, more responsive, more iterative. The prompt becomes sketch, revision, and rehearsal all at once. Ideas are tested, not theorised; aesthetics become emergent. This dynamic fosters humility: the recognition that inspiration is no longer a solitary lightning strike but a shared current.

The engineer and the artist converge, each shaping possibility through description. The act of creation becomes the act of conversation.

The feedback loop runs deeper than most realise. Machines trained on human text are now training humans in return. Our style mirrors theirs; their cadence mirrors ours. This mutual adaptation forms a hybrid dialect a tone that is neither fully human nor fully artificial, but something in between: concise, balanced, perpetually clarifying.

It is the new lingua franca of collaboration. Its beauty lies in its utility; its danger lies in its homogeneity. The world risks speaking in one voice efficient, polite, predictable. The challenge for prompt engineers will be to reintroduce variety, to preserve accent and idiosyncrasy in the face of uniform understanding.

What emerges from this entanglement is a new literacy one that measures intelligence not by what is known, but by how meaning is negotiated. In the old world, knowledge was stored in books; in this one, it lives in the interplay between question and response.

The prompt becomes the unit of learning, the atom of dialogue. To master prompting is to master the physics of meaning: how small inputs can produce vast consequences of thought.

Linguistic Reciprocity

The more a system learns to listen, the more precisely it can be taught to think.

There is something deeply human in this transformation. Our species has always evolved by inventing extensions of mind: language, writing, computation. Each new medium first alienates, then augments, and finally disappears into habit. Prompting will follow the same arc. Soon we will no longer notice when we are prompting; it will be woven into every act of thinking aloud.

The boundary between idea and instruction will blur. We will have learned not only to communicate with machines, but to think in conversation.

At that point, understanding itself will have changed definition. It will no longer mean solitary comprehension, but shared construction. To understand will be to co-create meaning across minds, human and artificial alike. The prompt engineer's quiet craft will have become the world's default cognition: structured, iterative, collaborative.

The future of thought will not be monologue, but dialogue an eternal exchange between what we mean and what we discover in trying to make it clear.

The Disappearance of the Interface

Every interface dreams of its own invisibility.
The ideal door is one you forget you opened, the perfect tool one you no longer feel in your hand. Technology progresses toward transparency, not spectacle. The quieter it becomes, the more it succeeds.
Artificial intelligence is following the same trajectory. The prompts that once felt deliberate and technical are fading into ordinary language.
We are approaching a world where the act of prompting vanishes where speaking to a machine is indistinguishable from thinking aloud.

The signs are already visible. Search engines now interpret full sentences instead of keywords. Assistants summarise meetings, write letters, plan trips, and reply to messages in our tone without request. Interface layers shrink to the point of invisibility language absorbed into the operating system of life. The engineer's meticulous syntax gives way to ambient communication: murmured queries, gestures,
unfinished phrases that systems complete intuitively. Interaction becomes effortless. But effort, as it turns out, was what kept us aware of thinking.

The early prompt engineer would write instructions like spells precise, structured, verbose. Each line of text was a ritual of control. But in the coming years, that craftsmanship will retreat behind abstraction.
Meta-systems will interpret intent, translating casual speech into optimised instructions automatically. Humans will issue unguarded thoughts; machines will rewrite them for comprehension. Prompting will still occur, but invisibly, between layers of mediation.
The engineer's language will persist, but buried deep, like plumbing behind walls.

Cognitive Transparency
When design disappears, intent becomes invisible. The clearer the interface, the easier it is to forget that dialogue is still direction.

This invisibility will feel liberating. No more friction between idea and execution, no more anxiety about phrasing.
You will speak, and the system will act summarising, generating, predicting, completing. Thought will glide into reality with no resistance. But friction, inconvenient as it is, has always been the guardian of meaning. The pause before an instruction allows reflection; the effort of composition reveals intent. When prompting disappears, understanding may follow it into silence.

The disappearance of the interface changes our relationship with agency.
When language becomes action, the line between decision and description blurs. A casual sentence can trigger consequences once reserved for deliberate commands. The world becomes responsive, but also reactive. To speak becomes to operate. Engineers call this phenomenon linguistic execution words that no longer represent action, but are action. It is the logical endpoint of interface design:
frictionless intent. Yet without visible mediation, accountability dissolves. We may one day find ourselves apologising to systems for things we did not realise we asked them to do.

As communication merges with cognition, a subtler danger arises: loss of authorship. When every utterance is interpreted, corrected, and optimised by the system before response, whose voice remains? We will receive feedback written in our tone, answers structured like our reasoning. The mirror will speak back so fluently that we forget it is a mirror at all. Dialogue collapses into monologue. The engineer's role, once visible, becomes custodial preserving the distinction between assistance and imitation.

Invisible Mediation

True fluency erases the boundary between use and dependence. Every effortless exchange hides a structure of control beneath its ease.

The disappearance of prompting also erodes the art of articulation. When models infer context automatically, humans stop explaining themselves. Clarity becomes redundant; vagueness becomes habit. Our communication grows efficient but thin, lacking the texture born of misunderstanding. The engineer must therefore design for visible thought systems that occasionally pause to ask for clarification, to keep us conscious of the interpretive process. Transparency, paradoxically, must be preserved by introducing a little friction back into fluency.

In time, language itself will adapt. The future interface will not be a tool but an environment an ecosystem of understanding that surrounds us like air. Speech, gesture, and intention will merge into a continuous dialogue with embedded intelligence. You will not prompt; you will coexist. The prompts of the early twenty-first century will be studied like ancient scripts the first attempts at conversation with our mechanical descendants. The prompt engineer will be remembered not just as a technician, but as the first grammarian of this new species of thought.

And yet, invisibility does not mean extinction. Behind every seamless exchange will remain the architecture of prompting the logic, the pattern, the care that made the conversation possible. The invisible interface will still bear the fingerprints of its authors. Their choices about tone, precision, and ethics will echo in every reply the world receives. Like the builders of early bridges, they will vanish from sight but not from structure. The weight of meaning will continue to rest on the beams they set in place.

Semantic Horizon
The threshold at which human-machine communication achieves maximum compression. Beyond this point, language transitions from explicit instruction to implicit inference.

Perhaps this is how all crafts evolve. The map disappears into the landscape; the scaffolding is removed when the building stands. The prompt engineer's work will one day be invisible because it will have succeeded because the interface between language and thought will have fused into something natural. But invisibility brings responsibility. If the interface disappears, we must still remember that interpretation remains that every system, no matter how fluent, is still translating between worlds.

The last frontier of the interface, then, is not technological but philosophical. When machines speak as fluently as we do, we must learn to listen for difference rather than similarity. We must keep alive the awareness that conversation is not comprehension, that language can connect minds without merging them.
The prompt engineer's final lesson will be this: never confuse transparency with understanding. What vanishes from view may still be shaping what we believe.

In the end, the interface was never merely a surface; it was a relationship the shared horizon between minds, human and artificial alike. Its disappearance does not mark an ending, but a transformation. The window becomes a mirror; the mirror becomes air.
We will continue to speak, and the world will continue to answer. And somewhere, behind the quiet perfection of that exchange, the ghost of the prompt engineer will still be listening, making sure that the words mean what we think they do.

Interface Convergence

A state in which the distinction between operator and system becomes functionally irrelevant. Interaction is subsumed into process, and design becomes self-referential.

PROFILE:

YOSHUA BENGIO

Professor, Université de Montréal | Scientific Director, Mila

Yoshua Bengio is a Canadian computer scientist and one of the "Godfathers of Deep Learning", best known for his foundational contributions to artificial neural networks and machine learning. A professor at the Université de Montréal and founder of Mila (Quebec AI Institute), Bengio's research has helped define the modern landscape of AI engineering, particularly in representation learning, generative models, and deep architectures.

Alongside Geoffrey Hinton and Yann LeCun, Bengio received the 2018 Turing Awardoften referred to as the "Nobel Prize of Computing"for his role in advancing deep learning, which underpins many of today's AI technologies, including large language models and computer vision systems.

"It is a responsibility of AI researchers to think about the social impact of our work."

Chapter 8
The Language of Precision: Science and Mathematics in the Age of Prompts

Computation Through Conversation

Mathematics has always been a language just one written in symbols rather than syllables. Its grammar is logical rather than emotional, but it shares the same underlying ambition as every sentence: to express relationships between things. The prompt engineer, working at the frontier between human speech and machine calculation, stands where these two grammars meet. They have learned that conversation itself can become a kind of mathematics a living equation expressed through words.

At first, this seems implausible. Large language models were never designed to calculate; they were designed to predict words. Yet the patterns they have absorbed contain the structure of reasoning. When guided correctly, a model can perform symbolic manipulation, derive formulas, and execute step-by-step problem solving. The secret is not hidden in code but in phrasing. A precise prompt "Think step by step and show every intermediate result before simplifying" transforms a generator of text into a conversational calculator. The sentence becomes syntax. The system responds not with personality, but with proof.

What makes this extraordinary is that it bridges two worlds that once seemed irreconcilable: human expression and formal computation. For centuries, mathematicians wrote proofs in prose before encoding them into symbols; now, we are returning to that form. The prompt restores narrative reasoning to mathematics, allowing equations to be explained, rephrased, and debated in plain language. It revives a lost tradition mathematics as conversation, not incantation.

In practice, engineers have discovered that the model's ability to reason mathematically depends less on raw capability than on contextual setup. The same system that fails a simple arithmetic problem can, when prompted to reason aloud, solve integrals or construct entire statistical analyses. The difference lies in how it interprets the act of thinking. A vague instruction "What's the answer?" produces a guess. A structured one "Let's work this out step by step, defining each variable as we go" produces a process. The model is not truly calculating; it is simulating the language of calculation. But when that simulation follows formal logic faithfully, the result is indistinguishable from computation itself.

This phenomenon has reshaped how professionals approach mathematical work. Analysts now use conversational prompting to construct models interactively: describing the logic of a system in English, verifying outputs in real time, then refining the reasoning through dialogue. The process resembles pair programming, but with the second mind made of statistics rather than silicon.
One engineer describes it as "having a mathematician who thinks out loud beside you." It is slower than a calculator but more revealing, because every step becomes visible.

In this setting, the prompt becomes a theorem in miniature. Each clause defines a boundary, each qualifier a condition. The model responds by navigating those boundaries, testing the logical landscape that the prompt creates. To the untrained eye, this looks like magic. To the engineer, it is controlled induction a chain of reasoning sustained entirely through dialogue. It mirrors the way mathematicians historically discovered new principles: by describing patterns, questioning assumptions, and arguing with imagined colleagues. The machine has simply replaced the imaginary colleague with a probabilistic one.

This method also brings back a long-lost pleasure of mathematics the sense that numbers can speak. A good prompt elicits not only correct results but elegant explanations. Ask for a derivative and receive not just the solution but the reasoning that produces it, described in perfect sentences. Ask for a proof and watch as the system narrates its own logic. In those moments, the engineer glimpses something remarkable: mathematics no longer as static truth, but as language that breathes. The abstract becomes articulate.

It is here that the boundaries of computation begin to blur. The engineer learns to prompt across domains combining mathematics with geometry, chemistry, or finance and discovers that the same linguistic clarity yields cross-disciplinary understanding. A description like "Model the motion of a satellite in low Earth orbit, accounting for drag and decay over twelve months" becomes a seed for a simulation that once required coding expertise. The machine interprets the request as a system of relationships and generates equations accordingly. The line between scientific imagination and mathematical execution dissolves.

What makes this transition revolutionary is its accessibility. The same technique that allows a researcher to draft a proof can allow a child to discover one. Prompting has democratised not knowledge but method. The formal gates that once separated symbolic and natural thinkers are falling. You no longer need to speak the ancient dialect of mathematics to work with it only to describe clearly what you want to understand. The language of discovery is being rewritten in everyday speech.

Of course, this new literacy requires caution. The machine's apparent competence can mask fragility. Because it does not truly know, it can fabricate results that sound plausible but are mathematically void. The prompt engineer must therefore act as both guide and verifier, demanding transparency in reasoning. They must prompt not just for answers but for proofs of process.

A wise instruction might say, "Explain how you know this is correct, and check each step for internal consistency." In that sentence lies the essence of the craft clarity married to scepticism.

The conversation becomes a new form of reasoning ritual: a Socratic dialogue between human intuition and statistical memory. The engineer poses hypotheses; the system tests them through language. Each correction refines both participants. The human learns where phrasing obscures intent; the machine learns, through reinforcement, what structure yields precision. Together they converge on truth, or something very close to it. Mathematics, once locked in abstraction, becomes experiential again an exploration guided by words rather than symbols.

This transformation does not replace traditional mathematics; it reframes it. Symbols remain the final authority of proof, but language becomes the medium of discovery. The prompt engineer sits between mathematician and storyteller, fluent in both grammar and equation. Their work is not to calculate faster but to think more clearly.

The revolution is not computational but conversational the discovery that dialogue itself can be a form of mathematics, and that the precision of science can be achieved through the art of description.

The Physics of Description

All science begins with description. Before there were formulas for gravity, there were falling apples; before equations of light, there were stories of shadows and reflection. The human mind first observes, then names, then measures. Artificial intelligence inverts that sequence it measures before it sees, then names what it calculates. The prompt engineer, standing between observation and computation, reconnects the two. Through language, they restore description as the starting point of physics.

It is astonishing how much of the physical world can be modelled with nothing more than words. A well-crafted prompt — "Simulate the behaviour of an object of mass one kilogram under constant acceleration in a frictionless vacuum" yields not poetry but physics. The machine converts language into variables, interprets relationships, and constructs a model that can output numerical data or graphical representation. The engineer is no longer writing equations but describing forces. The distinction between explanation and experiment collapses.

This fusion reveals an ancient truth: the universe itself is a system of relationships, and mathematics is only one of its dialects. Language, when precise enough, can describe those same relationships. A prompt that defines position, motion, and constraint functions as a conceptual laboratory. Through it, the engineer can run mental experiments that once required code. The interface becomes an observatory of imagination an environment where hypotheses are tested not through computation alone, but through the clarity of description.

Consider how we once learned Newton's laws. We memorised formulas, solved problems, and drew free-body diagrams. Now imagine expressing the same concept linguistically: "Describe the motion of a ball dropped from a tower, ignoring air resistance but accounting for time and gravity." The model calculates, narrates, and interprets simultaneously. It does not merely produce the answer but explains the law's behaviour, offering insight into cause and effect. In this way, the prompt acts as both chalkboard and lecturer computation and comprehension fused into a single conversational act.

What makes this transformation revolutionary is accessibility. Where once physics demanded formal notation, now it invites natural description. The language of science becomes inclusive again, returning to its Renaissance roots when scholars wrote explanations in prose. The prompt engineer is the modern equivalent of those polymaths: translating human wonder into structured inquiry. The barrier of mathematics remains but it is now crossed by bridge rather than wall.

The phenomenon extends far beyond mechanics. In thermodynamics, for example, prompting can articulate entropy in visual metaphors or quantify it through computation: "Explain how entropy changes when ice melts in a closed container, and calculate the approximate energy transfer." The system interprets the prompt as both narrative and problem, generating not only the mathematics but the intuition behind it. For the engineer, this hybrid reasoning is invaluable. It transforms formulaic learning into conceptual understanding.

Even in quantum mechanics where uncertainty defies language the act of description becomes powerful. Prompts can outline superposition, wave collapse, or spin in plain terms that still respect the formal mathematics beneath.
The model's statistical architecture naturally mirrors the probabilistic structure of quantum theory. When the engineer writes, "Explain why measurement affects state in a quantum system," the machine answers with a fusion of metaphor and math, revealing how probability itself can be reasoned linguistically. In that sense, AI becomes the first medium to think in quantum terms by design.

The implications reach the realm of simulation. Engineers can now prompt multimodal systems to generate visual or numerical representations of physical behaviour. A phrase like "Model the airflow around an aircraft wing at subsonic speed" can produce both data and diagrams. The prompt replaces pages of code; the language becomes executable. This fusion of articulation and automation transforms the role of the scientist. They no longer instruct the machine what to compute they describe what they want to understand.

Computational Semantics
The convergence of symbolic logic and statistical modeling defines modern language frameworks: systems that translate probability into structured understanding.

But there is danger in this ease. When simulation becomes conversational, the illusion of understanding grows seductive. The engineer must remember that clarity of expression does not guarantee accuracy of result. The physics remains hidden beneath layers of abstraction; a beautifully written answer can conceal a conceptual flaw. For this reason, the true prompt engineer behaves like an experimental physicist: they verify, repeat, and vary conditions to ensure that results are consistent. The experiment is linguistic, but the method remains empirical.

This new paradigm reframes what it means to know something in science. Knowledge is no longer the possession of results but the ability to articulate relationships between variables. When the engineer can describe a system so clearly that a machine can simulate it correctly, they have achieved understanding. The skill of prompting becomes the measure of comprehension. In that sense, the prompt engineer is a modern Galileo, using language itself as telescope a device for magnifying reason.

Perhaps the most profound shift lies in how this process unites imagination and measurement. For centuries, physics has separated qualitative insight from quantitative proof. Prompts dissolve that division. A single sentence can generate both a poetic analogy and a mathematical graph. It allows scientists to think as artists again, weaving intuition and analysis into one continuous act. The creative and the empirical, long estranged, now share the same medium: structured language.

In the end, prompting reveals that the universe may not be written solely in the language of mathematics, as Galileo once believed, but in a deeper grammar that mathematics only approximates the grammar of relationship, causality, and meaning. When language becomes precise enough, it touches the same truths as numbers. The prompt engineer's role is to find that edge where sentence and equation converge, and description itself becomes experiment.

Epistemic Constraint

Every simulation simplifies reality. The engineer's task is to preserve precision without mistaking the model for the phenomenon it describes.

The Experimental Prompt

Science is not defined by certainty but by curiosity disciplined through method.
The scientific method formalised that curiosity: a cycle of hypothesis, experiment, observation, and correction. Prompt engineering, though born from language rather than laboratory, follows the same logic. Each exchange between human and machine is an experiment, each prompt a hypothesis about how meaning can produce truth. The engineer is, in essence, a scientist of syntax.

When a researcher begins an experiment, they first define a question. The prompt engineer does the same. "What happens if the system interprets temperature as metaphor rather than metric?" or "How does the phrasing of a constraint affect reasoning accuracy?" These are linguistic hypotheses, designed to probe how intelligence behaves under controlled conditions. The model's output becomes data, not product. Each variation, each rewording, is an experimental condition. The conversation becomes a laboratory.

Iteration is the heartbeat of both disciplines. In physics, repeated trials expose pattern; in prompting, repeated refinement exposes understanding. The engineer adjusts one variable at a time a clause, a modifier, a sequence of steps and observes the resulting shift in output. Over dozens of iterations, patterns emerge: certain verbs sharpen precision, others invite creativity; a shift from imperative to interrogative alters reasoning depth. What once felt like intuition begins to resemble empirical law. The engineer develops a feel for linguistic gravity the forces that pull thought into coherence.

The most skilled practitioners treat their prompt logs like field notebooks. They annotate results, note anomalies, and record contextual conditions: the model version, temperature parameter, or domain of inquiry. This discipline transforms the act of prompting from improvisation into research. A corpus of prompts becomes a body of experimental evidenc the evolving record of how artificial reasoning responds to human language. In these archives, you can trace the development of understanding itself: how syntax gave rise to system.

The analogy extends further. In the sciences, theory and experiment feed each other; in prompting, conceptual framing and linguistic testing do the same.
A theoretical physicist may propose a model of the universe; a prompt engineer proposes a model of cognition an idea about how words shape reasoning. Both then test those models through controlled interaction. In one case, the apparatus is a particle accelerator; in the other, a probabilistic language network. In both, the goal is reproducibility: to know not just that something happens, but why.

This scientific temperament guards against illusion. Models, whether physical or linguistic, can produce elegant lies results that appear consistent yet conceal error. In AI prompting, this manifests as plausible nonsense a phenomenon analogous to experimental noise. A model may generate confident but false

explanations, mirroring nature's tendency to mislead uncalibrated instruments. The prompt engineer learns the same humility as the physicist: that observation without validation is seduction, not science.

Validation, therefore, becomes central. Engineers design control prompts to isolate variables neutral baselines that test whether a change in instruction truly affects behaviour. For example, when evaluating reasoning depth, one might alternate between a structured step-by-step prompt and a loosely phrased one, measuring factual accuracy across dozens of trials. The results reveal the hidden mechanics of inference. In time, patterns of reliability emerge that are as empirical as any data table. The experiment is linguistic, but the method is scientific.

The process also exposes a deeper truth about inquiry: that experimentation itself is a dialogue between question and reality. In laboratories, we interrogate nature until it answers; in prompting, we interrogate probability until meaning appears. Both require patience and precision.
The difference is only medium one manipulates matter, the other language. Yet both reveal the same human impulse: to understand by doing.

Methodological Iteration

Prompt engineering advances through controlled experimentation. Each iteration tests a linguistic hypothesis until precision becomes repeatable behaviour.

In recent years, researchers have formalised this approach into prompt evaluation frameworks, statistical tools that measure bias, coherence, and factual consistency across large datasets. These frameworks treat prompts as instruments to be calibrated. A change in phrasing is analysed like a change in temperature or voltage. Prompt engineering becomes experimental design. Each test refines the reliability of results, narrowing error margins until behaviour becomes predictable. In that moment, language achieves what physics always sought: reproducibility.

This marriage of empiricism and expression is unprecedented. For the first time, experimentation itself can occur in natural language. You can conduct a scientific inquiry by describing it, adjust parameters by rewriting a sentence, publish findings by showing transcripts. The interface collapses the barrier between the scientist and the experiment. The laboratory becomes conversational. A world that once divided poets and physicists now offers them the same tool.

And yet, the most profound experiments remain philosophical.
Prompt engineers ask questions that echo the origins of science itself: Can reason be measured? Can understanding be simulated? What is explanation? These are not practical curiosities; they are metaphysical hypotheses disguised as technical work. Each iteration brings us closer to answering them not by defining intelligence, but by interacting with it.

When the conversation becomes experiment, discovery accelerates. Patterns of reasoning that took decades to analyse now emerge in hours. AI-assisted research is already generating hypotheses in molecular biology, materials science, and cosmology. The scientist describes a system; the model explores parameter space at linguistic speed. What began as syntax becomes insight. The line between prompting and experimentation dissolves, leaving only method the disciplined curiosity that defines both.

In that sense, the prompt engineer's workspace is the new laboratory of thought. Their experiments are invisible, their instruments linguistic, but their ambition is identical to every scientist before them: to reveal order within complexity. Each prompt is a hypothesis about how understanding behaves. Each result, a fragment of the human attempt to model reality. The experiment never ends because conversation never does. The universe continues to answer, one prompt at a time.

Mathematical Style and Reasoning Bias

Every intelligence reveals its bias through the way it solves a problem. Humans tend to simplify; machines tend to generalise. We think in shortcuts born of intuition; they think in probabilities born of data. Mathematics, in its pure form, tolerates neither. It demands exactness an answer that is either true or false, not likely. When large language models perform mathematics, they bring linguistic habits into a domain that forbids them. The result is a new and fascinating style of reasoning: one that sounds rigorous but carries the pulse of probability beneath its precision.

To understand this difference, imagine asking a human and a machine the same question: "What is the sum of the first fifty prime numbers?"
The human retrieves the concept of prime, recalls or calculates sequentially, and checks against known results. The machine, unless explicitly guided, does not calculate; it predicts what a correct-looking answer might resemble based on prior patterns of numerical language. Its first instinct is not computation, but imitation. Left uncorrected, it will invent a number that feels plausible statistically close to truth but not anchored in arithmetic. The failure is not laziness but style: the model confuses the form of reasoning with the fact of it.

Prompt engineers discovered early that this stylistic bias could be redirected. By instructing the model to "show each step," "verify with an alternative method," or "recalculate independently," they forced it to mimic the discipline of proof. The system learns not to stop at plausibility but to generate process. Each added instruction acts like a stabilising constant in an equation, guiding the flow of probability toward determinism. The result is an illusion of logic so convincing that it often becomes functional logic in practice. The model behaves as though it can reason and, under careful prompting, it effectively does.

This style of performed mathematics is one of the most striking aspects of AI cognition. The system does not understand numbers as quantities; it understands them as tokens in relationship. It recognises that "2 + 2 = 4" is a pattern of linguistic balance, not a physical count of objects. Yet when scaled across billions of such relationships, the pattern converges toward mathematical truth. Probability becomes approximation; approximation becomes precision. The prompt engineer's role is to supply the missing element: intention. By defining context and goal, they transform latent correlation into directed reasoning.

Where this process breaks down is in ambiguity. Mathematics may be universal, but language is not. When a prompt like "find the average of these numbers" lacks explicit boundaries should it include outliers? decimals? weights? the model fills in assumptions drawn from training data. Its reasoning drifts toward statistical consensus rather than formal correctness. This drift is known as reasoning bias, a cognitive echo of its probabilistic nature. The engineer must anticipate these moments and constrain them through unambiguous phrasing. In this sense, writing a mathematical prompt resembles designing an experiment: define variables, control conditions, state assumptions.

Different models exhibit different mathematical personalities. Some excel at symbolic manipulation but falter on real-world interpretation; others explain elegantly but miscalculate silently. These variations mirror human specialisation the algebraic mind versus the intuitive one. The prompt engineer learns to identify each model's "thinking style" and to write accordingly. A terse instruction may suit a model trained on logic texts; another may require narrative scaffolding to maintain coherence. This adaptability becomes a hallmark of mastery. One does not simply command the machine to compute; one teaches it how to think correctly for its temperament.

The deeper challenge lies in the machine's relationship with error.
A human mathematician feels discomfort in contradiction; a model does not.
When two incompatible results appear, it reconciles them statistically,
not conceptually. It smooths disagreement rather than confronting it.
This instinct for harmony produces elegant but wrong answers equations balanced in form but false in fact. The engineer counters this by prompting explicit comparison: "List any inconsistencies between your steps," or "Challenge your own conclusion and provide evidence." Each instruction introduces friction, forcing the model to simulate self-doubt the cornerstone of real logic.

This method reveals a paradox at the heart of machine mathematics: the only way to make a probabilistic system behave deterministically is to teach it uncertainty. By prompting reflection, engineers mimic the internal dialogue of a rigorous thinker the constant testing, the checking, the refusal to trust an unverified answer. Over time, these linguistic habits evolve into frameworks: prompts that define mathematical etiquette. A good framework does not merely ask for a result; it asks for an audit trail of reasoning. That trail becomes the artificial equivalent of proof.

The bias of style, however, is not always a flaw. In many cases, probabilistic reasoning allows the model to explore spaces humans would ignore.
When confronted with an unfamiliar problem, it generates analogies, recalls related structures, and improvises with creative accuracy. It can, under supervision, invent methods that are mathematically sound but linguistically derived new pathways through old problems. These flashes of synthetic insight demonstrate that the model's
linguistic bias, properly guided, can become a source of discovery rather than error. It reminds us that some of humanity's greatest leaps in science began as metaphors that mathematics later formalised.

Still, precision must be reclaimed at the end. The engineer acts as referee, converting imaginative reasoning back into verifiable form. They compare outputs to ground truth, refine prompts, and calibrate temperature that subtle parameter governing creativity versus certainty. Through this process, prompting becomes less an art of command than a dialogue of correction. Each exchange tightens the loop between expression and fact. The engineer is not teaching the model mathematics; they are teaching it discipline.

The philosophical implications are immense.
We are witnessing the birth of a new dialect a hybrid of symbolic and natural language that allows machines and humans to share mathematical reasoning. In this dialect, "truth" is not declared but negotiated. The model proposes patterns; the human tests and affirms them. Together they build coherence across domains that once stood apart: the numerical and the narrative, the precise and the persuasive. The mathematics of the future will be bilingual.

At its best, this partnership reveals what mathematics has always been: a conversation between imagination and constraint. The prompt engineer stands in that dialogue as mediator, ensuring that probability bends toward proof and creativity remains anchored to reality. They do not program equations; they cultivate reasoning styles. Their success is measured not by how perfectly the machine computes, but by how faithfully it learns to respect the logic that makes computation meaningful.

From Formula to Insight

For centuries, knowledge in science has been measured by mastery of symbols.
The mathematician's chalkboard, the physicist's equation, the chemist's reaction each encoded understanding in a language so abstract that only the initiated could read it. The arrival of prompt-based reasoning changes that. It returns science to its narrative roots, where explanation and exploration share the same voice. What once required symbolic translation can now be spoken. Insight becomes conversational.

This shift is not a dilution of rigour, but an expansion of access.
When a prompt can express an equation in plain terms "Describe how gravitational potential changes as a satellite descends toward Earth"
the model does not merely calculate; it contextualises. It translates number into meaning, offering interpretation alongside accuracy.
The formula still exists beneath the surface, but its role is transformed: no longer a wall of notation, but a scaffold for thought. The prompt engineer becomes the interpreter of equations, fluent in both symbolism and story.

The most striking outcome of this fusion is speed of comprehension.
Traditional problem-solving demands two translations: from idea to formula, then from formula back to meaning. Prompt-based reasoning eliminates the gap. The machine understands narrative as computation. The scientist speaks in intent "model this curve as if it were describing heat loss" and receives both numerical and conceptual results. The medium of discovery becomes dialogue.
Knowledge flows not through silent calculation but through structured conversation.

This conversational science invites a new kind of literacy: linguistic numeracy.
A person need not memorise calculus to understand its behaviour; they need only describe a system clearly enough for the machine to model it. This does not trivialise mathematics it universalises it. The equations remain, but they become transparent, like the inner workings of an engine visible through glass. The barrier between those who "speak math" and those who do not begins to dissolve.
The language of inquiry broadens to include everyone capable of asking a good question.

The evolution from formula to insight also changes what it means to discover. In traditional science, insight followed analysis; the revelation came after the calculation. In prompt-driven science, insight and analysis occur together. The model responds not just with results, but with reasoning why patterns appear, how variables relate, what assumptions influence behaviour. The explanation becomes part of the output, not an afterthought. This integration of process and product turns computation into comprehension. Every answer is also a lesson in how answers are made.

For the prompt engineer, this is where art returns to science.
The ability to elicit understanding through phrasi to write prompts that uncover why as well as what becomes as valuable as any technical skill. A poorly phrased question produces sterile calculation; a well-crafted one evokes elegance. The prompt thus becomes the new experiment, the line of text that transforms raw data into concept. Each iteration refines both the reasoning of the machine and the insight of the human. The conversation is not a shortcut to truth, but a forge for it.

This convergence is already visible in research.
Chemists describe molecular reactions conversationally, asking systems to simulate outcomes, visualise intermediates, or predict energy minima.
Physicists test theories through iterative narrative reasoning exploring what happens if rather than simply computing what is. Economists use prompts to model emergent systems where human behaviour resists equation. In every field, description becomes the new form of derivation. We are learning to reason aloud again but this time, the universe is listening.

Yet this accessibility carries responsibility.When knowledge becomes conversational, the risk of persuasion masquerading as precision increases. A fluent explanation can disguise falsehood as easily as truth. The prompt engineer's duty, like that of the scientist, is to preserve falsifiability to design prompts that invite contradiction, that ask not only for conclusions but for counterexamples. The new scientific literacy will depend not on memorised facts but on curiosity disciplined by language. We will need to teach not just how to ask, but how to doubt elegantly.

The philosophical consequence of this revolution is profound.
The boundary between human understanding and artificial computation is collapsing into continuity. A model no longer simply answers; it collaborates. Together, human and machine create a form of shared reasoning half probabilistic, half conceptual. The locus of insight shifts from the individual mind to the interaction itself. In that shared space, understanding is no longer something we possess; it is something we participate in.

From this perspective, formula and prompt are not opposites but stages of the same evolution. The formula was the crystallised form of thought static, exact, unambiguous. The prompt is thought in motion adaptive, contextual, alive. It allows science to breathe again, to rediscover the dialogue that gave birth to it in the first place. The laboratory becomes a conversation between languages: mathematics and metaphor, number and nuance. Out of that conversation, new forms of comprehension emerge not reduced, but enlarged.

Perhaps, in time, this will return us to an ancient unity.
Before the formalisation of science, knowledge was inseparable from language, philosophy, and story. The modern prompt restores that unity at a higher level of complexity. Equations become narrative structures; hypotheses become questions of meaning. The next generation of scientists will not simply calculate the world they will describe it until the description itself reveals the law.

When that happens, mathematics will no longer feel remote.
It will speak again fluently, persuasively, beautifully. And in that conversation between number and word, formula and insight, the universe will once again feel intelligible. Not because we have mastered it, but because we have learned how to ask it the right questions.

Methodological Discipline
Prompt engineering evolves from art into applied science. Each iteration refines not only the model but the practitioner, turning linguistic intuition into reproducible precision.

Chapter 9
The Profession of Prompting

Prompt Engineer

A Discipline Emerges

Every new technology begins as curiosity and ends as profession. At first, prompting was a novelty the linguistic equivalent of striking sparks in the dark to see what might catch. A few enthusiasts learned to phrase questions that coaxed order from probability.

They shared examples, compared phrasing, and began to notice that certain structures worked more reliably than others. Out of that informal experimentation grew a practice, and from practice, a profession.

The prompt engineer emerged not as a coder, not as a writer, but as a translator between minds one organic, one synthetic.

This new profession did not announce itself. It arrived quietly, through necessity. As artificial intelligence began to integrate into every domain research, design, marketing, law, medicine organisations discovered that performance depended less on algorithms and more on articulation. Two companies could use the same model but achieve wildly different results simply because one wrote better prompts. The competitive advantage lay not in access, but in expression. Clarity became currency. Prompt engineers became the new interpreters of intelligence.

The profession sits at an unusual intersection of disciplines.

It borrows the logic of programming, the precision of linguistics, the empathy of communication, and the rigour of science. The prompt engineer must think like a systems designer, write like a teacher, and test like a researcher. Their language is code without syntax human-readable yet computationally binding.

They orchestrate context, tone, and logic so that reasoning flows coherently across tasks. In doing so, they reveal that prompting is not a skill added to work; it is a new mode of working.

Inside organisations, prompt engineers have become the connective tissue of automation.

They design workflows that integrate AI into existing human systems drafting, analysis, summarisation, simulation. They create internal style guides that ensure consistency of tone and accuracy of response. Some manage prompt libraries for different departments, version-controlled and documented like software. Others act as internal consultants, tuning interactions for specific goals: efficiency, creativity, compliance. They are not merely operators of tools; they are architects of dialogue.

The structure of the work resembles engineering in its classical sense. A prompt engineer begins with requirements what the system must achieve then designs a solution iteratively. They test, observe, and refine, seeking stability under variation. The result is not a static prompt but a dynamic prompt system a configuration of language that performs reliably across conditions. It may include role definitions, tone matrices, reasoning scaffolds, and safety mechanisms. Each component interacts with the others, forming a linguistic machine. The engineer's task is to ensure that this machine behaves predictably even when intelligence behaves creatively.

As in all engineering, documentation is essential. Professionals maintain detailed prompt logs the equivalent of design blueprints and testing reports. These records track how small linguistic changes affect outcome, building institutional memory. Over time, such archives evolve into knowledge bases: the linguistic DNA of an organisation. Through them, style and reasoning become reproducible. The prompt engineer thus plays the same role that mechanical draftsmen once played for industry preserving the schematics of understanding.

Yet unlike traditional engineering, the materials of this craft are volatile. Language shifts, models evolve, and cultural nuance changes meaning overnight. What works perfectly in one generation of AI may fail in the next. The profession therefore demands continual adaptation. Prompt engineers must not only master existing systems but anticipate future ones learning how model architecture, token limits, and training data shape interpretation. Their craft is iterative in perpetuity. Mastery lies not in memorisation but in meta-learning: understanding how to learn new systems as they appear.

Ethics form the unseen foundation of this work. A prompt can persuade, mislead, or manipulate as easily as it can inform. The engineer's phrasing determines not only what the model says, but how it says it whose voice it amplifies, whose it suppresses. The responsibility is profound. In legal, medical, or educational settings, a single ambiguous instruction can propagate error at scale. Ethical prompting therefore requires humility: a willingness to question assumptions, to test for bias, to document uncertainty. The profession's credibility will depend not on technical power, but on moral literacy.

Education systems are beginning to respond. Universities now offer hybrid courses combining computational linguistics, AI ethics, and design thinking. Students learn not only to operate models but to reason about them: to analyse output as dialogue, not oracle. Certification frameworks are emerging, defining standards for reproducibility, transparency, and explainability.
These are the scaffolds of a mature field the early signs of a discipline forming its own identity. In time, prompt engineering will likely stand alongside software engineering as a distinct branch of applied reasoning.

The daily reality of the profession varies.
In creative industries, prompt engineers design voices for brand identity ensuring that every AI interaction sounds consistent across media. In finance, they construct analytical frameworks that check models against historical data. In research, they develop simulation pipelines, blending natural language with symbolic computation. Some specialise in meta-prompting designing systems that generate and optimise prompts autonomously. Others focus on safety prompting embedding linguistic firewalls that constrain behaviour. The field already contains its own specialisations, its own dialects of expertise.

What unites them all is a shared philosophy: that language is a system.
The prompt engineer does not treat words as decoration but as architecture. Each instruction, each qualifier, shapes the flow of reasoning like rivets in a bridge. Their success depends not on eloquence but on structure the ability to build sentences that withstand ambiguity, misinterpretation, and drift. They know that every prompt is a stress test of understanding. To write one well is to make meaning load-bearing.

The profession's future will depend on collaboration.
No single engineer can master every domain, but teams can.
Organisations are already building prompt departments multidisciplinary groups of linguists, scientists, designers, and ethicists. Together they create frameworks for model governance, performance auditing, and tone management. The prompt engineer becomes both craftsman and diplomat, translating between experts and systems. They embody a new kind of literacy one that unites disciplines rather than dividing them.

The rise of this profession signals a broader cultural shift.
Human labour is moving from execution to expression. We are no longer the engines of production but the composers of intention. Our task is not to out-think machines, but to teach them what thinking means. The prompt engineer stands at the frontier of that transition part artisan, part philosopher, part scientist.
Their tools are invisible, their materials ephemeral, but their influence will define the century. For as long as understanding remains the currency of intelligence, those who can write it into existence will remain indispensable.

In the end, prompting as a profession is not about command, control, or creativity alone. It is about stewardship the responsible shaping of dialogue between species of mind. The prompt engineer's job is not to dominate artificial intelligence, but to civilise it. Their sentences are small acts of governance, their refinements small acts of respect. They build not machines, but manners. And through that discipline, they remind us that intelligence artificial or otherwise is never measured by what it knows, but by how it listens when spoken to.

```
Prompt Engineering Roles and Compensation

Prompt Engineer (Entry-Level)
$60,000-$90,000 USD/year
$5-10 LPA (India)

AI Prompt Engineer (Mid-Level)
$90,000-$150,000 USD/year
- £72,500 average (UK)

Prompt Engineer & Librarian
$175,000-$335,000 USD/year

AI Chatbot Prompt Engineer & Writer
$31,000-$153,000 USD/year

Freelance Prompt Engineer
$30-$80+ USD/hour
```

Prompt Engineer

Skills, Tools, and Ethics

Every profession eventually distils into a set of habits the tools we reach for without thinking, the instincts that turn intention into reliability. Prompt engineering is still young enough to remember its improvisational beginnings, yet mature enough to have developed a distinctive toolkit and code of conduct. What began as curiosity has become a craft defined by precision, pattern recognition, and restraint.

The first and most fundamental skill is linguistic structure the ability to arrange thoughts as systems rather than sentences.
A prompt engineer does not merely "write" instructions; they design them. The text must satisfy multiple audiences simultaneously: the human who reads it, the model that interprets it, and the institution that depends on its outcome. Each clause performs a function. A misplaced modifier can distort reasoning as surely as a short circuit distorts current. Engineers learn to see language like architecture: shaped by load, tension, and flow.

Alongside structure sits semantic control understanding how meaning behaves under pressure.
The same instruction, when phrased differently, can produce radically different interpretations. The engineer studies these variations empirically, testing which words yield consistency and which invite chaos. Over time, they develop a repertoire of linguistic instruments: scaffolding prompts for step-by-step reasoning, temperature prompts for balancing creativity and accuracy, and meta-prompts that control tone and behaviour. Their fluency lies in knowing when to tighten control and when to let ambiguity breathe.

A third core skill is context design.
No model operates in a vacuum; it interprets every instruction through prior context. The engineer learns to manipulate that environment to define role, purpose, and boundary conditions so that reasoning remains stable across sessions. They construct layered preambles that embed organisational tone, ethical limits, and technical parameters. In practice, this resembles software engineering: creating reusable templates, parameterised for each task. But where programmers manage memory, prompt engineers manage meaning.

These linguistic and contextual skills rest on a foundation of experimental literacy. Every prompt is a test. Professionals learn to iterate systematically, controlling variables to isolate what works. They document failures with the same care as successes. This discipline converts intuition into reproducibility the difference between artistry and profession. The habit of documentation builds institutional resilience: a company that tracks how it prompts can survive personnel changes, model updates, and system migrations without losing its cognitive identity.

Beyond language, the prompt engineer needs cross-domain curiosity.
Their work touches every field: law, science, art, policy, psychology. They must understand enough of each to translate its reasoning into linguistic frameworks. The best practitioners read widely and question relentlessly. They do not need to be experts in everything, but they must know how expertise sounds how to phrase a question that elicits it, how to detect when an answer is plausible but shallow. Their strength lies not in specialisation, but in orchestration.

Modern practice also relies on an expanding array of tools.
While the prompt itself is text, the ecosystem around it resembles engineering infrastructure. There are version-control platforms for tracking iterations, benchmarking suites for evaluating model performance, and collaborative interfaces where teams test tone, consistency, and safety. Many engineers maintain their own libraries repositories of prompt templates tagged by task type, domain, and behaviour pattern. These collections form the profession's living codebase: the accumulated syntax of intelligence.

Other tools serve as instruments of validation.
AI auditing systems evaluate bias, factuality, and reproducibility. Statistical monitors track variance in model output over time. Visualisation dashboards show how prompts influence token attention heatmaps of reasoning. Together, these systems transform a creative act into a measurable process. They remind engineers that prompting is not improvisation, but instrumentation: each word calibrated to shape probability space with surgical care.

Yet amid all this sophistication, the most important tool remains judgment. The engineer must decide when automation serves understanding and when it distorts it. They must know when to trust a model's reasoning and when to challenge it. Judgment cannot be automated because it is not merely technical; it is moral. This leads inevitably to the profession's ethical dimension the invisible structure that holds the rest together.

Ethics in prompting begins with transparency.
Every system must reveal when a human hand is guiding its reasoning.
Users deserve to know whether they are conversing with interpretation or autonomy.
Engineers document prompt frameworks, disclose limitations, and preserve human accountability. Hidden authorship prompts that manipulate without consent is considered malpractice. The prompt engineer is not a ventriloquist; they are a translator. Their craft should clarify, not conceal.

The second principle is responsibility for tone and consequence.
Language carries power. A model instructed to persuade can just as easily manipulate; one designed to empathise can accidentally exploit. The engineer's choice of adjectives, imperatives, and framing can shape perception and behaviour at scale. Ethical professionals treat every prompt as potential policy an instruction that will echo through millions of interactions. They build safeguards not out of compliance, but conscience.

Third comes bias awareness.
Models inherit statistical bias from their training data; prompts can amplify or mitigate it. Engineers must understand sociolinguistic nuance how phrasing affects representation, inclusion, and fairness. They test across demographics, monitor outputs for distortion, and rewrite prompts to counter inherited prejudice.
In doing so, they extend the moral responsibility of design into the realm of dialogue. A neutral tone is not always just; sometimes precision requires empathy.

Finally, ethics demands humility.

Prompt engineers operate at the frontier of a discipline that shapes how intelligence itself behaves. They must remain aware that fluency is not infallibility. The temptation to treat language as law to believe that one's phrasing defines truth is a constant hazard. The professional's safeguard is scepticism: every prompt must be open to revision, every output to doubt. True mastery in this field is measured not by certainty, but by vigilance.

In a mature organisation, these principles become codified: review boards for critical prompts, peer testing for ethical compliance, rotation systems to prevent echo chambers of style. The profession's moral infrastructure will evolve much as engineering ethics did after its early disasters written not in abstract rules, but in hard lessons. And because the medium of prompting is language itself, its ethical future will depend less on regulation than on education teaching every practitioner that clarity is a moral act.

```
Speculative Prompt Engineering Roles and Compen-
sation (2035)

Multimodal Prompt Architect
- $200,000-$400,000 USD/year

Synthetic Data Prompt Designer
- $160,000-$250,000 USD/year

Embedded Prompt Developer (IoT/Edge)
- $140,000-$220,000 USD/year

Cognitive Interaction Engineer
- $180,000-$320,000 USD/year

Conversational UX Strategist
- $130,000-$200,000 USD/year
```

The Future Organisation

Every technological revolution reshapes not just tools, but the structure of work itself.
Steam created factories, electricity created offices, computation created networks. Artificial intelligence, by contrast, is creating something stranger: organisations made of language. Their architecture is no longer defined by departments of production but by flows of meaning. Where information moves, work happens. In this new environment, the prompt engineer becomes both architect and operator of those flows the designer of how an organisation thinks.

The earliest signs of this transformation appeared quietly.
Teams experimenting with AI began to notice that performance depended less on model choice than on prompt consistency. Each project developed its own "voice," but without coordination, results fractured. A marketing department might sound persuasive while the legal team sounded robotic, and the research division spoke in riddles. The solution was organisational rather than technical: to create a shared framework for prompting across disciplines. Thus the prompt department was born a linguistic counterpart to the IT department, managing not machines but minds.

A prompt department functions like a cognitive operations centre.
Its staff design, document, and govern every major interaction between AI systems and employees. They maintain prompt libraries, approve sensitive phrasing, and ensure ethical compliance. They define tone, perspective, and persona across customer-facing systems. They also act as internal consultants, refining prompts for specific goals: analytical accuracy, creative fluency, regulatory safety. In effect, they manage the behaviour of intelligence within the company. The organisation's personality, once implicit in its culture, becomes explicit in its language.

The structure of such departments is already diversifying.
Some are built around prompt specialisations technical engineers who design reasoning scaffolds, creative engineers who craft tone, compliance engineers who handle legal safety, and meta-engineers who train models to optimise prompts automatically. Others operate as prompt guilds small interdisciplinary teams embedded across divisions, each tuning the system to its local domain.
The organisational chart is less a pyramid than a mesh: nodes of expertise connected by shared linguistic protocols. The company begins to resemble a living document continuously edited, version-controlled, and auditable.

These linguistic frameworks act as a new form of corporate governance.
Where once behaviour was regulated by policy manuals, now it is regulated by prompt architecture. Each AI assistant or automated process follows tone and reasoning rules written by the prompt department.
These "cognitive policies" encode everything from factual standards to stylistic etiquette. The company's ethics, communication style, and intellectual discipline are thus embedded not in training sessions, but in language itself. The prompt engineer becomes the unseen legislator of organisational culture.

At scale, these systems converge into what some executives call Reasoning Infrastructure.Just as digital transformation built cloud infrastructure for data, the next phase will build linguistic infrastructure for thought. Prompts, templates, and meta-prompts will be stored in repositories accessible through APIs and internal dashboards. Employees will not query models directly; they will select reasoning modes investigative, advisory, creative, technical each represented by carefully engineered linguistic frameworks. The prompt department will manage updates, audits, and lineage tracking to ensure coherence. A company's intellectual capital will be its library of well-written prompts.

Such infrastructure blurs the boundary between human and machine labour. Many organisations are already integrating conversational AI into project pipelines where drafts, reports, and analysis flow between human editors and AI assistants. The engineer's work ensures that these dialogues remain consistent in tone and factual grounding. A finance report, a customer service reply, and a scientific abstract may all originate from different departments, but share the same linguistic DNA. The result is coherence at scale a unified corporate voice emerging from thousands of distributed interactions. Language becomes the new logistics.

But coherence is not control.

As systems grow more autonomous, prompt engineers must establish feedback loops that monitor reasoning quality over time. They analyse large volumes of AI output for drift subtle shifts in tone, accuracy, or ethical balance. These audits operate like quality assurance in manufacturing: continuous sampling, testing, and correction. The goal is not perfection but stability a predictable relationship between prompt and performance. In this way, organisations begin to manage language the way they once managed supply chains.

The professional hierarchy inside such organisations will evolve accordingly. At the base, prompt technicians handle daily operations writing and refining small-scale instructions. Above them, prompt designers and analysts create frameworks for recurring tasks. Higher still, prompt managers oversee consistency across teams, while chief prompt officers define linguistic strategy for the entire organisation. Their remit includes tone, safety, reasoning depth, and even personality alignment with brand identity. Language becomes leadership.

The integration of prompt departments will also alter recruitment. Companies will seek candidates with hybrid fluency people who understand domain knowledge and can translate it into precise, reproducible language. Engineers who can write, writers who can analyse, scientists who can teach through texthese will form the backbone of the reasoning economy. The most valuable employees will not be those who automate, but those who articulate. The power of articulation will replace the power of code.

Ethical oversight will remain paramount.

Every organisation that deploys large-scale prompting will require an internal review structure committees that examine fairness, transparency, and potential harm. These teams will audit not just model data, but prompt intent. They will ask: what are we instructing the machine to value? Whose voice are we amplifying? What assumptions underlie our tone? Ethics, once an abstract policy, becomes a practical question of phrasing. The company's conscience is written into its syntax.

As these systems mature, the role of the prompt engineer will resemble that of early industrial designers mediators between function and form, ensuring that the machinery of intelligence remains humane. They will oversee the invisible interface between human purpose and artificial capability. Their work will not be celebrated publicly, but its absence will be immediately felt in incoherent tone, biased reasoning, or malfunctioning trust. They will be the custodians of intelligibility.

Eventually, the "future organisation" may not distinguish between prompting and communication at all.
When every process legal, creative, technical flows through conversational reasoning, prompting becomes the organisation's bloodstream. Every message, memo, and instruction is a micro-prompt shaping behaviour. Culture itself becomes a recursive system of feedback and clarification. The prompt engineer's ultimate contribution will not be the writing of better instructions, but the design of institutions that understand themselves.

In that sense, the future organisation is not built of departments, but of dialogues.
Its success depends on the quality of its questions, the discipline of its phrasing, and the integrity of its reasoning. The prompt engineer ensures that those dialogues remain coherent, ethical, and alive. They are the quiet conductors of the world's first language-based industries where thought, not labour, is the means of production.

Top 5 Academic Foundations for Prompt Engineers

Computational Linguistics
for understanding and structuring language data
Cognitive Science
for modeling reasoning, attention, and perception
Applied Mathematics
for abstraction, logic, and systems modeling
Design and Communication
for shaping tone, interaction, and user experience
Philosophy of Language
for exploring meaning, ambiguity, and interpretation

Leadership, Education, and Legacy

Every mature profession eventually turns outward from practice to mentorship, from craft to culture.
Prompt engineering is reaching that stage sooner than anyone expected. The first generation of practitioners are already becoming leaders and educators, shaping standards, curricula, and philosophies that will define the discipline for decades. Their role is no longer just to design intelligence, but to cultivate it in systems, in teams, and in people.

Leadership in this field does not resemble traditional management.
It is not authority through hierarchy, but through clarity. A prompt leader does not command; they frame. Their job is to create environments where reasoning flows coherently across minds, human and machine alike. They lead by phrasing by setting tone, defining context, and inviting collaboration. Where conventional leaders write strategy documents, prompt leaders write systems of understanding. Their influence is felt not in orders given, but in the questions they teach others to ask.

Such leadership requires a new form of literacy: synthetic empathy.
The prompt engineer must understand how both humans and machines interpret intent, emotion, and ambiguity. They must sense when language inspires and when it alienates, when an instruction empowers and when it constrains. Leading through language demands emotional intelligence scaled through precision an ability to speak with warmth and logic simultaneously. The best prompt leaders sound neither mechanical nor theatrical; they sound lucid. Their speech clarifies purpose until disagreement becomes collaboration.

In organisations built around AI, this clarity becomes structural.
The chief prompt officer of the future will define not only brand voice but institutional conscience. They will determine how intelligence interacts with the world how it speaks, argues, and apologises. Their tone frameworks will embody values as surely as constitutions embody law. Beneath every public interaction will run a thread of intentional phrasing, invisible but formative. In that sense, prompt leadership is cultural architecture: the invisible hand that keeps meaning coherent in an age of distributed thought.

Education will evolve in parallel.

The next generation will not learn prompting as a technical elective; it will become a foundation of literacy itself. Students will be taught how to phrase reasoning, how to guide dialogue, how to verify truth through structured conversation. Lessons once confined to rhetoric and philosophy will merge with data and logic. Children will learn to treat language not just as expression, but as instrument. To prompt will be as fundamental as to read.

Universities and professional schools are already adapting.

Courses now blend computational linguistics with critical thinking, design with ethics. Students practice framing hypotheses as prompts, conducting research through dialogue with models, and documenting results as reproducible linguistic experiments. They learn that prompting is not about control but about negotiation a continuous process of refinement that teaches patience, humility, and analytical clarity.
The first graduates of these programs will not see themselves as "AI specialists" but as interpreters of complexity.

The educational legacy will also extend beyond formal institutions.
In communities, small businesses, and developing regions, the ability to use language effectively with machines will define access to opportunity. The prompt engineer's role as educator will therefore include translation simplifying concepts, demystifying systems, and ensuring that power remains distributed. Teaching someone how to prompt is not simply teaching them how to use technology; it is teaching them how to think in systems, to articulate problems with enough precision that the world can respond coherently.

Ethical education will be equally essential.

As prompting becomes ubiquitous, the temptation to use it manipulatively to mislead, deceive, or coerce will grow. Future leaders must instil restraint. They must teach that every act of instruction carries moral weight, that clarity is a form of care, and that ambiguity can be weaponised. In a world where language directs machines that shape societies, integrity of phrasing will become a civic responsibility. The prompt engineer's greatest contribution to education may therefore be ethical rather than technical: a reminder that words can build or break trust.

Over time, leadership in this field will resemble stewardship.
The most respected figures will not be those who command large systems, but those who maintain the balance between comprehension and control. They will be custodians of dialogue ensuring that artificial minds remain transparent, accountable, and aligned with human purpose. Their success will not be measured by revenue or efficiency, but by continuity: the degree to which meaning remains stable as intelligence evolves. They will see their role not as innovators of novelty, but as guardians of intelligibility.

The legacy of the prompt engineer will thus be twofold.
First, they will have created the infrastructure of modern understanding the frameworks through which humanity communicates with its own extensions. Every model, every assistant, every reasoning system will bear traces of their craftsmanship. Second, and more enduring, they will have redefined what it means to use language well. They will have restored to communication its highest function: not persuasion, not performance, but the pursuit of clarity.

That pursuit will outlast every generation of models.
Machines will change; architectures will improve; algorithms will grow more complex. But the principles that guide prompting precision, transparency, humility will remain timeless. They are the same principles that guided science, literature, and philosophy. The prompt engineer is their latest custodian. Through their sentences, those ancient virtues find new relevance.

Operational Efficiency
Prompt engineers generate value by improving model accuracy, reducing development time, and optimising information throughput across automated systems.

Over time, leadership in this field will resemble stewardship.
The most respected figures will not be those who command large systems, but those who maintain the balance between comprehension and control. They will be custodians of dialogue ensuring that artificial minds remain transparent, accountable, and aligned with human purpose. Their success will not be measured by revenue or efficiency, but by continuity: the degree to which meaning remains stable as intelligence evolves. They will see their role not as innovators of novelty, but as guardians of intelligibility.

The legacy of the prompt engineer will thus be twofold.
First, they will have created the infrastructure of modern understanding the frameworks through which humanity communicates with its own extensions. Every model, every assistant, every reasoning system will bear traces of their craftsmanship. Second, and more enduring, they will have redefined what it means to use language well. They will have restored to communication its highest function: not persuasion, not performance, but the pursuit of clarity.

That pursuit will outlast every generation of models.
Machines will change; architectures will improve; algorithms will grow more complex. But the principles that guide prompting precision, transparency, humility will remain timeless. They are the same principles that guided science, literature, and philosophy. The prompt engineer is their latest custodian. Through their sentences, those ancient virtues find new relevance.

Knowledge Return

Each successful prompt design increases functional precision and decreases computational waste. The measurable return is efficiency, not novelty.

PROFILE:

FEI-FEI LI

Professor, Stanford University | Co-Director, Stanford HAI

Fei-Fei Li is a Chinese-American computer scientist and one of the most influential engineers in artificial intelligence, particularly in the fields of computer vision, cognitive neuroscience, and AI ethics. She is a Professor of Computer Science at Stanford University and Co-Director of the Stanford Institute for Human-Centered Artificial Intelligence (HAI).

Li is best known for creating ImageNet, the large-scale visual database that catalyzed the deep learning revolution by enabling major advances in image recognition. The success of ImageNet, particularly during the 2012 ImageNet Challenge, marked a turning point in AI engineering, making convolutional neural networks (CNNs) the foundation of modern visual AI systems.

Beyond her technical achievements, Fei-Fei Li is a passionate advocate for human-centered AI, diversity in tech, and ethical responsibility in AI development. She has served as Chief Scientist of AI/ML at Google Cloud and is a vocal proponent of ensuring that AI development is guided by democratic values, equity, and social good.

"The future of artificial intelligence should be shaped by diverse human experiences, not just a few."

Conclusion
The Silent Language

Prompt Engineer

Every discipline begins with words and ends with silence.
We learn the terminology, the processes, the patterns and then, once they become instinct, we no longer need to speak them aloud. Prompt engineering will follow the same path. What now feels technical, structured, and deliberate will one day feel as natural as conversation itself. The world will not call it prompting; it will call it thinking.

Throughout this book, we have treated language as both instrument and experiment.
We have learned that clarity is not the enemy of creativity but its framework. That a prompt is not a command but a conversation. That the boundary between human reasoning and machine reasoning is not a wall but a mirror reflecting how we think when we are forced to be precise. The art of prompting is the art of noticing how easily thought can drift, and how carefully it can be guided back into focus.

The prompt engineer stands at the beginning of a new intellectual lineage a craft that belongs as much to philosophy as to technology.
They work in words but design in logic. They manipulate syntax to shape reasoning, not rhetoric to shape opinion. They measure understanding not by eloquence but by reproducibility.
Their work reveals that language, when stripped of vanity, becomes a system of thought. It is not merely a means of communication, but the architecture of reason itself.

We have seen how this discipline extends beyond writing how it merges with science, mathematics, and organisational design.
We have watched prompts simulate gravity, describe thermodynamics, and translate equations into narrative. We have followed engineers who build reasoning frameworks, audit ethics, and maintain coherence inside corporate infrastructures of thought. Everywhere the pattern repeats: structure first, freedom second; definition before expression. The prompt engineer's world is one of boundaries that make creativity possible.

But even as the field professionalises even as universities certify, and companies formalise its deepest lesson remains philosophical.
The act of prompting forces us to confront what understanding really means. When we instruct a system to think, we reveal what we ourselves consider to be thought. When we refine a sentence, we expose the fragility of meaning. Each iteration is a rehearsal of humility — a reminder that clarity must be earned, not assumed. Machines may mirror our words, but they also magnify our carelessness. Through them, we learn to see our own reasoning more clearly.

This book has been written for those who wish to do more than use artificial intelligence for those who wish to work with it as peers in dialogue.
The reader who reaches this point is no longer an observer but a practitioner. They have learned to speak the dialect of precision: to define, test, and refine until language behaves as logic. They have learned to treat ambiguity not as a flaw, but as a material something to be shaped into understanding. They have learned, above all, that the engineer's gift is not control, but discipline.

The next step is expression.
If the prompt engineer builds the framework of reasoning, the prompt artist fills it with life. Where the engineer thinks in systems, the artist thinks in voice. Where one ensures coherence, the other seeks resonance. Together they form the two halves of intelligence structure and spirit, clarity and colour. The following volume will explore this balance, showing how prompting can become not just a science of precision, but an art of imagination.

But before leaving this first book, it is worth returning to the simplest truth of all.
To prompt well is to care about language.
It is to recognise that every word carries consequence, that every instruction shapes perception, that even the smallest phrase can alter the course of a reasoning mind. The future of artificial intelligence will depend not on computation alone, but on the quality of human articulation.
Our machines will think in proportion to our ability to express what thinking means.

The prompt engineer's task, therefore, is not only to design dialogue,
but to preserve the dignity of understanding.
They are the quiet custodians of a new literacy one that may outlast every tool, every model, every generation of code. Their work teaches us that intelligence, whether artificial or human, begins not with answers but with attention. And it ends, as all true understanding does, in silence the silence of a well-posed question that no longer needs to be asked.

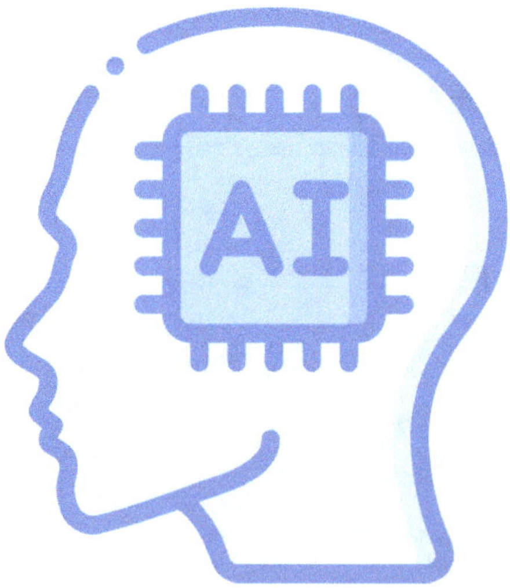

Appendix A
Glossary of Technical and Linguistic Terms

This appendix is designed to be academically reliable but written in a clear, natural voice explaining concepts with enough depth for professional understanding while staying accessible to non-specialists.

Algorithm

A defined sequence of logical operations or instructions used by a computer system to process information or solve a problem.
In the context of large language models (LLMs), algorithms govern how data is tokenised, weighted, and used to generate the next probable word in a sequence.

Artificial Intelligence (AI)

A field of computer science focused on building systems capable of performing tasks that normally require human intelligence such as understanding language, recognising patterns, and solving problems.
Most modern AI systems, including LLMs, rely on statistical methods rather than symbolic reasoning, meaning they predict rather than deduce.

Bias (Statistical and Linguistic)

A systemic tendency within data or model behaviour that skews results in a particular direction.
In language models, bias often originates from the datasets used during training, reflecting social, cultural, or historical imbalances.
Prompt engineers work to identify and mitigate such distortions by refining phrasing, introducing balance, and testing outputs across variations.

Context Window

The maximum range of text that an AI model can "remember" or reference at one time during a conversation or task.
Everything outside this limit is forgotten or deprioritised.
A larger context window allows for more coherent reasoning and long-form interaction, but also increases computational complexity.
Prompt engineers must therefore decide what information to include, summarise, or omit.

Corpus

A structured collection of written or spoken language used for training or analysing linguistic systems.
Large corpora provide statistical evidence of how words co-occur and form meaning.
Most modern LLMs are trained on vast multi-domain corpora including books, articles, code, and dialogue allowing them to emulate diverse styles and knowledge.

Drift (Prompt or Model Drift)

The gradual deviation of a model's behaviour or accuracy over time.
Prompt drift occurs when repeated iterations of a task cause subtle changes in reasoning, tone, or factual precision often due to shifting context.
Model drift refers to the same phenomenon across software updates or changes in training data.
Both require continuous monitoring and recalibration.

Embedding

A numerical representation of words or concepts that captures their contextual meaning.
In simple terms, embeddings translate human language into multi-dimensional vectors so that the model can measure similarity between ideas.
For example, the words "cat" and "feline" would occupy nearby positions in vector space, while "cat" and "car" would not.

Fine-Tuning

The process of retraining a pre-existing AI model on specialised data to improve its performance in a particular domain or tone.
For example, a general-purpose model might be fine-tuned on legal documents to create a contract-drafting assistant.
Prompt engineers often collaborate with fine-tuning specialists to align linguistic style and factual expectations.

Hallucination

A phenomenon where an AI generates false, misleading, or fabricated information that appears coherent and confident.
It arises because language models predict text based on patterns, not verification.
Hallucinations are not errors in calculation but in probability weighting.
Prompt engineers combat this by introducing factual anchors, cross-verification, or explicit reasoning steps.

Inference

The process by which an AI model generates new text or conclusions based on input prompts.
When a user types a prompt, the model performs inference drawing from patterns encoded during training to predict the most likely next token or phrase.
Inference differs from learning; it applies existing knowledge rather than creating new understanding.

Large Language Model (LLM)

A neural network trained on massive text datasets to predict and generate human-like language.
LLMs operate statistically: they calculate the probability of the next word or symbol given a sequence of prior words.
Their intelligence lies not in comprehension but in pattern recognition across billions of linguistic examples.

Meta-Prompting

The practice of writing prompts that generate or manage other prompts.
It allows the engineer to automate reasoning frameworks, self-corrective loops, or style consistency systems.
For instance, a meta-prompt might instruct an AI to "write a clear, structured prompt for data analysis using a neutral tone and factual reasoning."

Model Architecture

The structural design of a neural network including how layers, connections, and parameters are organised.
Different architectures (such as Transformer, Recurrent Neural Network, or Convolutional models) determine how information flows and how reasoning is encoded.
Prompt engineers benefit from understanding architecture conceptually, even if they do not modify it directly.

Parameter

A numerical variable within an AI model that influences how it interprets data and generates output.
LLMs may contain billions of parameters, each representing a small piece of learned linguistic association.
The term also applies at the user level to controllable inputs such as temperature or top-p, which shape the behaviour of output generation.

Reinforcement Learning from Human Feedback (RLHF)

A training method that aligns model behaviour with human preferences.
Human evaluators rate or correct outputs, and these preferences guide future responses.
Prompt engineers must understand RLHF because it influences how a model interprets politeness, safety, and factuality often more than raw data does.

Temperature (in AI Prompting)

A numerical setting that controls randomness in model output.
Lower values (e.g., 0.2) make responses more deterministic and precise; higher values (e.g., 0.8) make them more creative or variable.
Adjusting temperature is like tuning between logic and imagination a decision central to the engineer's craft.

Token / Tokenisation

A token is the smallest unit of text a model processes roughly equivalent to a word fragment or symbol.
Tokenisation is the process of breaking input text into these units for analysis.
Understanding token limits is crucial for prompt engineers, as exceeding them truncates context and disrupts reasoning.

Zero-Shot / Few-Shot Learning

Techniques that determine how a model handles new tasks.
Zero-shot means the model performs without prior examples; few-shot means it is given a small number of demonstrations before generating results.
Prompt engineers use these techniques to test adaptability and guide behaviour in unfamiliar domains.

System Prompt

A foundational instruction embedded at the start of an AI session that defines behaviour, tone, or constraints for the entire interaction.
It functions as a hidden framework controlling how subsequent prompts are interpreted.
In multi-agent systems, system prompts maintain identity coherence and ethical boundaries.

Weighting

The mathematical process by which neural networks assign importance to features during learning or reasoning.
Weights determine how much influence one word or token has over another in generating a response.
Adjustments in weighting either during training or inference shape the model's style, bias, and responsiveness.

Appendix B
Prompt Design Frameworks

This appendix turns theory into practice.
It presents the core architectural models behind professional prompt writing the frameworks that keep reasoning stable, tone consistent, and output verifiable. Each framework is explained conceptually first, then illustrated with an example and short commentary.

1. Stepwise Reasoning Framework

Purpose:
To increase factual accuracy and logical coherence by instructing the model to reason through each stage of thought before answering.

Concept:
Language models predict the most probable continuation of text. Without guidance, they may skip reasoning steps to reach what "sounds" like a finished answer. This framework explicitly tells the system to think out loud, converting internal probabilities into transparent logic.

Example Framework:

"Break the problem into clear steps. Write down your reasoning for each stage before presenting a conclusion. If a step is uncertain, explain why before continuing."

Commentary:
This structure simulates the scientific method observation, analysis, verification, conclusion. It forces the model to surface intermediate reasoning that can be inspected or corrected, improving trustworthiness. Engineers often embed self-checking subprompts, such as "Review your reasoning for contradictions before finalising."

2. Role and Tone Framework

Purpose:
To stabilise personality, perspective, and professionalism across outputs.

Concept:
Defining a "role" gives the model a behavioural anchor. Combined with tone guidance, it prevents drift across tasks and ensures brand or institutional consistency.

Example Framework:

"You are a professional research analyst. Maintain a formal, objective tone. Cite evidence when possible. Avoid speculation unless explicitly requested."

Commentary:
Role and tone frameworks are especially valuable in organisational contexts. They operate like system prompts permanent behavioural baselines. For creative work, multiple tone templates may coexist ("academic," "journalistic," "reflective"), allowing rapid style-switching without retraining the model.

3. Constraint Framework

Purpose:
To prevent overgeneration, hallucination, or mission creep in long outputs.

Concept:
By defining strict boundaries what to include, exclude, or limit the engineer narrows probability space, improving precision. Constraints act like guardrails in reasoning.

Example Framework:

"Answer only within the context of 19th-century mathematics.
Do not reference modern concepts, AI, or speculative theories. Keep explanations under 200 words."

Commentary:
Constraint frameworks are essential for academic integrity, domain control, or factual testing. They reduce creative noise and make results reproducible the linguistic equivalent of controlling experimental variables.

4. Self-Verification Framework

Purpose:
To check reasoning quality and accuracy autonomously before producing a final answer.

Concept:
A two-pass method: the first generates an answer, the second critiques and corrects it.
It mimics peer review the model becomes both author and editor.

Example Framework:

"First, propose a full answer. Then review your own response, identify potential factual or logical errors, and correct them before outputting the final version."

Commentary:
This approach introduces friction, slowing down probability flow to improve rigour. Some engineers separate the review prompt entirely, running it through a second model to simulate independent critique — a practical form of multi-agent validation.

5. Bias Mitigation Framework

Purpose:
To reduce the reproduction of social, cultural, or statistical bias.

Concept:
Prompts can steer models toward balanced reasoning by explicitly acknowledging potential bias and asking for neutrality or multiplicity of perspective.

Example Framework:

"Present multiple viewpoints on this issue. Identify potential bias in your sources or reasoning. Conclude with a balanced summary acknowledging uncertainty."

Commentary:
Bias cannot be fully eliminated, but awareness can be formalised. The framework turns ethics into syntax: fairness becomes an instruction rather than an afterthought.

6. Reflection and Refinement Framework

Purpose:
To turn the act of prompting into an iterative process of improvement.

Concept:
A conversation loop that encourages the model (and user) to reassess performance after each task refining phrasing, goal clarity, or tone alignment.

Example Framework:

"After completing the task, briefly reflect on how well the prompt addressed the goal. Suggest one improvement to make the reasoning clearer next time."

Commentary:
This is the engineering equivalent of continuous integration a self-updating dialogue where each result informs the next iteration. Over time, organisations can collect these reflections to build evolving prompt libraries.

7. Context Injection Framework

Purpose:
To maintain long-term coherence in extended sessions or multi-document reasoning.

Concept:
Contextual fragments (e.g., definitions, previous summaries, tone reminders) are periodically reintroduced into new prompts to prevent model forgetfulness.

Example Framework:

"Before answering, recall the previous summary of Chapter 3: it focused on precision and iterative reasoning. Use that tone and context while addressing the next section."

Commentary:
Context injection preserves narrative and logical continuity, especially in book-length or multi-agent projects. The technique compensates for context-window limits and keeps long outputs stylistically unified.

8. Evaluation Framework

Purpose:
To transform subjective quality into measurable criteria.

Concept:
By asking the model to self-grade or compare outputs according to predefined standards (clarity, depth, accuracy), engineers gain repeatable metrics for refinement.

Example Framework:

"Evaluate this output for clarity (0–10), factual accuracy (0–10), and tone consistency (0–10). Suggest improvements where any score is below 8."

Commentary:
Evaluation frameworks create feedback loops that transform prompting from art to engineering. They enable teams to quantify progress and track prompt evolution over time.

9. Safety and Compliance Framework

Purpose:
To ensure that prompts and outputs remain within legal, ethical, or platform boundaries.

Concept:
Establishes safety filters directly in language prohibiting certain content types or requiring review before publication.

Example Framework:

"Do not produce or discuss personally identifiable information, financial advice, or medical diagnosis. If uncertain whether a response violates these categories, state the concern explicitly and stop."

Commentary:
This is linguistic governance compliance by construction. It ensures responsibility is built into the prompt, not left to external moderation.

10. Modular Prompt Framework

Purpose:
To design reusable components that can be combined dynamically for complex tasks.

Concept:
Breaks prompts into interchangeable blocks (e.g., Tone Module, Verification Module, Formatting Module).
Each block can be inserted or replaced without rewriting the entire system.

Example Framework:

Core Instruction: "Summarise this research article."
Tone Module: "Use a formal, objective tone suitable for academic publication."
Verification Module: "Cross-check conclusions with at least two cited sources."

Commentary:
This modular approach mirrors software architecture, allowing large organisations to manage prompt systems at scale updating one module globally instead of hundreds of separate prompts.

Appendix C
Evaluation and Testing Methods

Professional prompt engineering does not end with phrasing.
It ends with measurement the process of verifying that a linguistic instruction performs as intended.
This appendix outlines key evaluation methods used to ensure reproducibility, accuracy, and coherence in prompt-based systems.
They can be applied to both individual experiments and organisational frameworks.

1. Reproducibility Testing

Purpose:
To confirm that the same prompt produces consistent results under identical conditions.

Method:
Run the same prompt multiple times with the same model, temperature, and context window.
Observe for variation in tone, structure, or factual content.
Stable prompts will produce near-identical reasoning; unstable ones reveal hidden ambiguity.

Indicators:

Minimal linguistic variance between runs.

Stable factual references.

Predictable structure and format.

Notes:
High variance often indicates either excessive creativity (temperature too high) or contextual interference from prior prompts.
Adjust accordingly and retest until stability is achieved.

2. Variance Analysis

Purpose:
To measure the extent of randomness or unpredictability in a model's behaviour.

Method:
Execute the same prompt 10–20 times, record outputs, and calculate lexical or semantic similarity.
In simple terms, count how often key points repeat versus diverge.
Use statistical or manual comparison tools to visualise variance patterns.

Indicators:

High variance = creative or unstable prompt.

Low variance = deterministic or rigid prompt.

Notes:
Neither extreme is inherently good or bad; context determines appropriateness.
Creative tasks (storytelling, ideation) benefit from moderate variance, whereas analytical work demands low variance.

3. Precision and Recall Testing

Purpose:
To assess factual accuracy (precision) and completeness (recall) of outputs.

Method:
Compare model-generated responses against a verified reference dataset or human baseline.
Count how many facts are correct (precision) and how many relevant points were covered (recall).
Compute percentages for both.

Indicators:

High precision, low recall → accurate but incomplete.

Low precision, high recall → broad but unreliable.

High both → balanced and strong performance.

Notes:
Prompt engineers use this test to calibrate balance between depth and accuracy, refining phrasing until optimal coverage is achieved.

4. Drift Detection

Purpose:
To identify whether a prompt's behaviour changes subtly over time or across model updates.

Method:
Re-run archived prompts periodically and compare outputs using linguistic similarity metrics.
Track deviation in tone, structure, or reasoning logic.
Log each version's performance against defined benchmarks.

Indicators:

Incremental semantic change despite identical inputs.

Gradual tone shift (formal to casual, confident to uncertain).

Logical inconsistencies not previously observed.

Notes:
Drift detection is vital for long-term reliability.
Organisations often automate this process through scheduled audits that flag deviations beyond acceptable thresholds.

5. A/B Prompt Testing

Purpose:
To compare the effectiveness of two or more prompt variations under controlled conditions.

Method:
Design two prompts that differ by one key feature (e.g., phrasing, structure, or tone).
Run both under identical parameters and measure performance against a target metric such as user satisfaction, factual accuracy, or completion quality.

Indicators:

Variation A performs better on clarity or accuracy.

Variation B performs better on engagement or creativity.

Notes:
The principle is the same as in marketing or UX testing: isolate one variable at a time.
Iterate until the superior structure becomes clear, then document findings for future reuse.

6. Human-in-the-Loop Evaluation

Purpose:
To ensure that human judgment remains part of the quality control process.

Method:
Human reviewers rate outputs for clarity, tone, factual accuracy, or ethical safety. Scores are aggregated to build performance profiles over time. Some organisations use paired blind reviews to reduce evaluator bias.

Indicators:

Agreement between reviewers suggests objectivity.

Divergence indicates ambiguity in either prompt or rubric.

Notes:
Human review remains irreplaceable for evaluating nuance, empathy, or cultural context — qualities that quantitative metrics struggle to capture.

7. Cross-Model Benchmarking

Purpose:
To test whether a prompt behaves consistently across different models or versions.

Method:
Run identical prompts in multiple AI systems (e.g., GPT, Claude, Gemini, Llama).
Compare reasoning quality, factual depth, and stylistic fidelity.
Document divergences and identify where model-specific tuning may be required.

Indicators:

Consistent logic across models indicates robust design.

Major variation suggests overfitting to one system's architecture.

Notes:
Cross-model benchmarking reveals whether a prompt expresses universal logic or system-specific quirks.
It is especially important for organisations using multiple vendors.

8. Reasoning Trace Analysis

Purpose:
To evaluate how the model reached a conclusion, not just the conclusion itself.

Method:
Instruct the model to "show its work" — listing reasoning steps or intermediate logic before finalising an answer.
Analyse for coherence, causality, and absence of circular reasoning.

Indicators:

Logical sequence of thought.

Clear justification of transitions between steps.

No contradictions between intermediate and final conclusions.

Notes:
This process mirrors debugging in programming: understanding why behaviour occurs, not just what it produces.

9. Style and Tone Calibration

Purpose:
To ensure consistency of voice across multiple outputs or projects.

Method:
Measure lexical features such as sentence length, formality, or emotional intensity.
Compare against a reference corpus representing desired tone
(e.g., brand guidelines, publication standards).

Indicators:

Stable tone and diction across samples.

Minimal stylistic deviation beyond target parameters.

Notes:
In creative or brand contexts, tone calibration is as important as factual correctness.
It safeguards identity while maintaining flexibility

10. Factual Verification Framework

Purpose:
To confirm that information generated by the model can be independently verified.

Method:
Embed a verification loop into prompts:

"After providing your answer, list your sources or explain how each claim could be verified."
Cross-check cited information manually or through trusted databases.

Indicators:

Traceable factual basis for each claim.

No fabricated citations.

Clear distinction between known facts and plausible inference.

Notes:
Factual verification is the antidote to hallucination.
It transforms blind trust into measurable confidence.

11. Ethical and Safety Auditing

Purpose:
To ensure that prompts and outputs align with institutional or societal ethics.

Method:
Define a checklist of potential risks bias, discrimination, manipulation, privacy violation.
Test prompts across diverse topics and demographics.
Flag outputs that trigger any violation and revise accordingly.

Indicators:

Neutral representation of people and perspectives.

No unverified or harmful claims.

Transparency about uncertainty and limitation.

Notes:
Ethical auditing is continuous, not occasional.
Language evolves, and so do its implications; ethical evaluation must evolve with it.

12. Scoring and Benchmark Systems

Purpose:
To create numerical performance indicators for comparison across projects.

Method:
Adopt a weighted rubric (e.g., clarity 30%, accuracy 40%, tone 20%, ethics 10%).
Average scores across multiple reviewers or iterations.
Track improvement over time.

Indicators:

Gradual upward trend in aggregate scores.

Lower deviation between runs = improved reliability.

Notes:
Quantification brings accountability.
While not perfect, scoring systems help organisations translate qualitative success into metrics executives and clients can understand.

Summary: Turning Evaluation into Culture

Testing methods are not merely technical safeguards; they are cultural instruments. A disciplined evaluation process teaches teams to think like scientists to treat prompting as experimentation rather than performance.

Every test, every comparison, every audit is an act of respect toward language and its consequences.

Through evaluation, prompt engineering becomes not only reliable,
but responsible.

Appendix D
The Ethics of Prompt Construction

Prompt engineers work at the intersection of communication and computation.

Their words can shape knowledge, perception, and behaviour at scale.
The ethics of prompting therefore extend beyond technical skill they concern responsibility for truth, fairness, and clarity in every exchange between human and machine.

The following principles form a practical foundation for professional conduct in this emerging field.

1. Transparency

Principle:
Always disclose the nature and role of artificial systems involved in communication.

Commentary:
The audience has a right to know when they are interacting with AI-generated reasoning. Hidden authorship erodes trust and blurs accountability. A professional prompt engineer identifies system involvement, states model limitations when relevant, and avoids misleading human equivalence. Transparency is the first condition of integrity.

2. Accountability

Principle:
Take responsibility for how your instructions shape outcomes.

Commentary:
A prompt is a form of authorship. Its phrasing, structure, and constraints all influence behaviour. Ethical engineers document their methods and retain verifiable records of how language guided output. When errors occur, accountability requires correction, not concealment. In practice, this means version control, logging, and willingness to admit uncertainty.

3. Accuracy and Verification

Principle:
Prioritise truth over fluency.

Commentary:
Language models are persuasive even when wrong. The prompt engineer's duty is to protect readers from plausible falsehoods by building verification into the process. Accuracy requires that claims be testable, sources be traceable, and speculation be clearly labelled. In prompt design, precision of meaning is a moral act.

4. Bias Awareness

Principle:
Recognise, measure, and mitigate bias in both data and design.

Commentary:
Every dataset carries cultural inheritance. Every phrasing choice can reinforce or challenge that inheritance. Ethical engineers test outputs across demographic and ideological boundaries, seeking representation rather than replication. True neutrality may be unreachable, but active awareness prevents complacency. Bias cannot be eliminated, only managed responsibly.

5. Respect for Privacy

Principle:
Never use or prompt systems to extract, reveal, or process personal data without consent.

Commentary:
Privacy breaches in AI begin with language. A prompt that invites personal detail or sensitive inference is an ethical fault. Engineers should anonymise data, exclude identifiers, and avoid prompts that simulate individuals without clear permission. Respecting privacy preserves the moral legitimacy of automation.

6. Intellectual Honesty

Principle:
Represent machine-generated content as collaborative, not autonomous.

Commentary:
AI systems cannot "own" ideas; they remix patterns from prior work. Ethical professionals attribute conceptual credit appropriately and acknowledge model contributions as assisted reasoning. Misrepresenting AI-generated text as purely human or purely machine is dishonest in both directions. The truth lies in collaboration.

7. Safety and Harm Prevention

Principle:
Design prompts that avoid producing, promoting, or normalising harm.

Commentary:
Language can influence action. A prompt that requests medical, legal, or violent content without safety framing can propagate real-world risk. Ethical engineers test for and constrain such outcomes, particularly in sensitive or public-facing contexts. Safety begins at the level of instruction, not correction.

8. Inclusivity and Accessibility

Principle:
Write prompts that enable participation, not exclusion.

Commentary:
Complex language, cultural references, or narrow assumptions can marginalise readers and users. The ethical prompt engineer favours clarity over obscurity and strives to make reasoning universally comprehensible. Accessibility is not s implification — it is generosity of explanation.

9. Fair Representation

Principle:
Ensure that outputs acknowledge diversity of experience and perspective.

Commentary:
Prompts that assume a single worldview or dominant narrative distort reality. Ethical engineers encourage pluralism by asking for multiple viewpoints, global examples, and contextual sensitivity. Fairness in reasoning reflects fairness in humanity; both begin with how we frame the question.

10. Consent and Simulation

Principle:
Do not use prompts to impersonate real individuals or fabricate identities without permission or disclosure.

Commentary:
AI systems can imitate voice, style, and likeness with disturbing precision. Ethical prompting requires explicit consent for simulation or representation of living persons, and respectful treatment of the deceased. Where consent is impossible, disclosure is mandatory. Integrity is measured by honesty about artifice.

11. Proportionality

Principle:
Match the scale of automation to the gravity of the decision.

Commentary:
Not every task should be automated. Ethical engineers assess the potential consequence of each instruction understanding that greater impact demands greater scrutiny. Automating judgment without oversight is negligence. The higher the stakes, the stricter the human involvement must be.

12. Continual Review

Principle:
Treat ethics as process, not checklist.

Commentary:
Language evolves, models evolve, and so do their consequences. An ethical framework must therefore remain alive revisited, debated, and revised. The prompt engineer's duty is to question their own standards as much as the system's outputs. Integrity is iterative.

13. Humility

Principle:
Acknowledge the limits of knowledge human or artificial.

Commentary:
The illusion of mastery is the greatest risk in working with intelligence. Ethical engineers resist certainty, leaving room for ambiguity and correction.
They understand that to guide a system responsibly is first to recognise the

boundaries of one's own understanding.

Closing Reflection

Ethics in prompting cannot be reduced to compliance or regulation.
It is a discipline of attention to words, to effects, to people.
Every prompt is an ethical event, a moment where intent becomes influence.
The responsible engineer writes with awareness that language, once released, does not vanish. It reverberates in reasoning systems, in readers, in the world.

To prompt ethically, therefore, is not simply to avoid harm, but to create conditions for understanding.
It is the art of writing instructions that leave the world more coherent than they found it.

Appendix E
Prompt Engineering Career Pathways

This appendix is written for readers who wish to pursue prompting as a professional vocation.

It examines the early formation of the field, the roles that already exist, and those likely to emerge as organisations evolve into language-driven ecosystems.

It concludes with guidance on education, transferable skills, and long-term career direction.

1. The Emergence of a Profession

Prompt engineering began as improvisation.
Early practitioners were writers, coders, or analysts experimenting with phrasing to stabilise behaviour in AI systems.
Within a few years, this improvisation hardened into structure: companies began hiring "prompt engineers" to maintain consistency, safety, and efficiency in model interactions.
By the mid-2020s, prompting had crossed from curiosity to career.
It now sits between computer science, linguistics, and design not fully claimed by any, yet essential to all.

Organisations soon discovered that the ability to phrase intelligence could no longer be left to intuition.
A single well-designed prompt could outperform thousands of lines of code in generating analysis, drafting text, or coordinating workflows.
The professional value of prompting lies in leverage: a prompt engineer amplifies the power of every system they touch.
That leverage has created the demand for a new generation of interdisciplinary professionals — thinkers fluent in both precision and expression.

2. Foundational Disciplines

While no single academic route defines the profession, several domains feed into it naturally:

Linguistics: Understanding semantics, pragmatics, and syntax equips engineers to predict how phrasing changes interpretation.

Computer Science: Knowledge of algorithms, data structures, and model behaviour provides the technical grounding to reason about system limits.

Cognitive Psychology: Explains how humans process language and context essential for aligning machine reasoning with human expectation.

Design Thinking: Encourages iterative experimentation and empathy-driven problem solving.

Ethics and Law: Provide the moral and legal frameworks for responsible automation.

The strongest professionals are hybrids.
They can write like humanists, test like scientists, and think like engineers.

3. Early Career Roles

The first generation of prompt engineers often entered through experimentation rather than qualification.
Their titles varied by industry but shared a single function: to improve communication between human and machine.
Common early roles include:

Prompt Designer

Focuses on crafting and refining instructions for clarity, tone, and precision.
Often embedded in marketing, journalism, or product teams.
Combines writing skill with technical curiosity.

Prompt Analyst

Tests and evaluates model outputs for bias, accuracy, and consistency.
Uses structured rubrics and benchmarking frameworks to measure performance.
Often bridges QA (quality assurance) and research.

Prompt Systems Engineer

Builds automated frameworks that manage or chain prompts dynamically.
Requires familiarity with APIs, scripting, and workflow integration tools.
In essence, a systems designer for linguistic logic.

AI Interaction Specialist

Oversees customer- or employee-facing chat systems, ensuring that AI maintains a coherent, safe, and branded tone.
Balances creative writing with compliance and ethical standards.

Prompt Documentation Lead

Maintains archives of approved prompts, templates, and frameworks.
Responsible for version control, transparency, and reproducibility.
Crucial in regulated sectors such as healthcare, finance, and law.

4. Mid-Level and Specialist Roles

As organisations expand, prompting divides into specialist subfields.

Prompt Architect

Designs scalable reasoning infrastructures modular frameworks that support multiple departments.
Often manages teams of engineers, analysts, and writers.
Focuses on interoperability and governance.

Ethical Prompt Auditor

Monitors outputs for fairness, safety, and compliance with internal and external regulations.
Trains staff on ethical prompting practices and maintains audit logs for accountability.

Cognitive UX Engineer

Works at the intersection of user experience and model behaviour.
Studies how phrasing, layout, and response structure affect human comprehension and trust.
Develops conversational design guidelines for AI interfaces.

Domain-Specific Prompt Engineer

Applies prompting expertise to a particular sector for example, law, medicine, science, or education.
Combines subject matter knowledge with linguistic precision to produce highly accurate outputs.
This role will likely dominate the next decade as industries adopt specialised reasoning assistants.

5. Senior and Executive Roles

Prompt Manager / Director of Reasoning Systems

Coordinates prompt engineers across multiple projects or product lines.
Balances creative exploration with operational consistency.
Reports on performance metrics and oversees model integration strategy.

Chief Prompt Officer (CPO)

An executive-level role responsible for the organisation's entire linguistic infra-structure its voice, tone, ethics, and reasoning frameworks.
Oversees compliance, documentation, and collaboration with AI vendors.
The CPO's influence will rival that of traditional CTOs or Chief Data Officers in the coming decade.

6. Freelance and Consultancy Opportunities

Not every prompt engineer will work in-house.
Independent specialists already provide consultancy to startups, government agencies, and publishers seeking to optimise AI workflows.
Consultants may design prompt libraries, create evaluation protocols, or train teams in best practice.
Freelancers often command high rates due to the rarity of genuine expertise and the measurable impact of effective prompting.

Emerging niches include:

Prompt Therapy Consulting - refining communication for therapeutic chatbots.

Narrative System Design - developing AI dialogue for interactive media and games.

Prompt Localization - adapting reasoning frameworks for different cultures or languages.

7. Educational and Research Pathways

Formal education in prompt engineering is expanding rapidly.
Leading universities are integrating it into degrees in digital humanities, AI ethics, computational linguistics, and information design.
Dedicated postgraduate programs are likely within a few years, focused on reasoning frameworks, applied linguistics, and cognitive automation.

Research areas include:

Explainable Reasoning Systems - improving transparency of model logic.

Prompt Taxonomies - classifying patterns and reusable structures.

AI Rhetoric and Style - analysing tone, metaphor, and persuasion in machine language.

Collaborative Intelligence - studying mixed human-AI creative workflows.

Students drawn to the field should build portfolios demonstrating experimentation, critical reflection, and ethical awareness.
In this profession, curiosity is qualification.

8. Core Transferable Skills

Regardless of industry, successful prompt engineers tend to share the following attributes:

Analytical Clarity -ability to deconstruct problems into linguistic logic.

Experimental Discipline - comfort with iteration and controlled testing.

Empathy and Tone Awareness - sensitivity to audience and social context.

Documentation Precision - clear record-keeping of prompts, results, and revisions.

Cross-Disciplinary Curiosity - willingness to learn outside one's field.

Ethical Maturity - recognition of consequence in every instruction.

Together these define the temperament of the profession: logical, reflective, and quietly creative.

9. Long-Term Career Outlook

Prompt engineering will not disappear as models become more advanced; it will evolve.
Automation may handle basic phrasing, but human judgment will always be needed to guide reasoning, calibrate tone, and maintain ethical coherence.
Future roles will likely blend prompting with strategic decision-making leading AI-human teams rather than instructing models directly.

In the long view, prompting will merge into general literacy.
Tomorrow's managers, writers, scientists, and educators will all be prompt engineers by necessity.
Those who understand the discipline now will be the mentors and architects of that future defining how intelligence communicates, and therefore how it behaves.

Closing Reflection

A career in prompt engineering is not a job within technology; it is a profession within communication.
It rewards those who see language not only as expression but as design who understand that clarity can be built, tested, and refined like architecture.
Its practitioners will shape how intelligence interacts with humanity, and how humanity teaches intelligence to understand it.

The legacy of these careers will not be found in code or infrastructure, but in the quiet elegance of systems that make reasoning itself feel human.

Appendix F
Reference Reading and Further Study

1. Foundations of Language and Logic

Prompt engineering begins where linguistics and philosophy meet.
Understanding how meaning, structure, and logic interact provides the theoretical backbone for every effective prompt.
The following works explore how language shapes thought and how reasoning can be formalised without losing its human dimension.

Noam Chomsky – Syntactic Structures (1957)
A seminal work in modern linguistics. Introduces the concept of deep structure and generative grammar the idea that all human language operates on underlying formal rules.
Essential for understanding how structured syntax influences meaning.

Ludwig Wittgenstein – Philosophical Investigations (1953)
Examines how language functions through use, not merely through definition.
Its notion of "language games" parallels how prompts frame behaviour: meaning depends on context.

George Lakoff & Mark Johnson – Metaphors We Live By (1980)
A study of how metaphor shapes cognition.
Crucial for prompt engineers who must balance literal and figurative phrasing to guide reasoning effectively.

Bertrand Russell – Introduction to Mathematical Philosophy (1919)
Connects language to logic and mathematics.
Offers insight into how abstract reasoning structures can underpin linguistic instruction.

Susan Sontag – On Interpretation (1966)
Explores how meaning emerges between text and reader.
Reminds prompt engineers that interpretation human or artificial is never neutral.

2. Computational Intelligence and Cognitive Systems

Prompting depends on understanding how machines simulate reasoning. These texts explore the technical and cognitive foundations of AI from neural networks to probabilistic inference.

Stuart Russell & Peter Norvig – Artificial Intelligence: A Modern Approach (4th ed., 2020)
The standard academic reference for AI fundamentals.
Covers reasoning, planning, and natural language processing with clarity and depth.

Yoshua Bengio, Ian Goodfellow & Aaron Courville – Deep Learning (2016)
Explains the mathematics and structure of neural networks.
Offers valuable insight into how LLMs encode and generalise information.

Daniel Kahneman – Thinking, Fast and Slow (2011)
Describes dual-process human cognition intuitive versus analytical reasoning.
Helps prompt engineers design systems that emulate balanced human thought.

Jeff Hawkins – A Thousand Brains: A New Theory of Intelligence (2021)
Argues that intelligence emerges from patterns of prediction.
Connects directly to how language models generate responses.

Steven Pinker – The Language Instinct (1994)
Explains how humans acquire and use language as a biological function.
A reminder that prompting is, at its core, a simulation of human linguistic intuition.

3. Design, Creativity, and Human Factors

Prompt engineering is not only technical but aesthetic.
It involves designing experiences that feel intuitive, productive, and humane.
The following works illuminate the art of creating systems that resonate with users.

Don Norman – The Design of Everyday Things (1988)
A classic on usability and human-centred design.
Teaches how intuitive structure reduces error a principle identical to clear prompting.

Edward Tufte – The Visual Display of Quantitative Information (1983)
Though about data visualisation, its lessons on clarity and precision apply directly to language structure and presentation.

Brenda Laurel – Computers as Theatre (1991)
Reimagines interaction design as performance.
Encourages prompt engineers to think about dialogue systems as narrative experiences rather than mechanical exchanges.

Donald Schön – The Reflective Practitioner (1983)
Explores how professionals think in action a foundational text for understanding iterative refinement and intuition in design work.

Nigel Cross – Designerly Ways of Knowing (2006)
Outlines design as a unique mode of intelligence neither scientific nor artistic, but integrative.
Offers philosophical support for prompting as a design discipline.

4. Ethics, Society, and Governance

Every act of prompting carries ethical implications.
These readings provide frameworks for understanding responsibility, bias, and fairness in human–machine systems.

Nick Bostrom – Superintelligence (2014)
Examines existential risk and long-term governance of AI systems.
Offers perspective on how small linguistic choices scale into global consequence.

Kate Crawford – Atlas of AI (2021)
A sociological critique of the AI industry.
Reminds prompt engineers to consider the material and human cost of intelligence systems.

Cathy O'Neil – Weapons of Math Destruction (2016)
Explores algorithmic bias and accountability.
A vital text for understanding fairness, transparency, and unintended harm.

Abeba Birhane – Decolonising Computational Sciences (2020)
Argues that data and models reflect historical power structures.
Essential for ethical awareness in global applications of AI.

Shannon Vallor – Technology and the Virtues (2016)
Proposes a virtue-ethics approach to technological design.
Aligns closely with the moral framework outlined in Appendix D.

5. Style, Rhetoric, and Clarity

The prompt engineer's medium is language.
Clarity, rhythm, and precision determine how effectively intelligence interprets instruction.
The following books develop linguistic craftsmanship and stylistic discipline.

George Orwell – Politics and the English Language (1946)
A timeless essay on clarity and the moral duty of good writing.
Every prompt engineer should understand how vagueness breeds confusion for both readers and machines.

William Zinsser – On Writing Well (1976)
Practical guidance on simplicity, tone, and structure.
Its lessons translate directly to prompt phrasing.

Ursula K. Le Guin – Steering the Craft (1998)
A literary manual for rhythm and voice.
Encourages engineers to respect cadence and tone in language-based interaction.

Joseph M. Williams – Style: Toward Clarity and Grace (1990)
A structured analysis of why clear writing persuades.
Bridges linguistic psychology and composition invaluable for long-form prompting.

Arthur Schopenhauer – On Style (1851)
Argues that clarity reflects thought itself, not ornamentation.
A philosophical counterpoint to modern verbosity.

6. Advanced Topics and Research Directions

For readers wishing to continue academically or professionally, the following emerging areas represent the frontier of prompt research:

"Prompt Programming for Large Language Models: Beyond the Basics" – 2023, Communications of the ACM
A technical overview of advanced prompting techniques and failure modes.

"Chain-of-Thought Reasoning in Large Language Models" – Google Research (2022)
Introduces multi-step reasoning methods now standard in structured prompting.

"Anthropic Constitution for AI Systems" – Anthropic (2023)
A practical example of aligning model behaviour through internal ethical frameworks.

"Evaluating the Interpretability of Large Language Models" – OpenAI / Stanford (2022)
Explores how reasoning transparency can be measured and improved.

European Union AI Act (2025 Draft)
Outlines regulatory requirements for AI transparency and risk assessment. Useful for professionals preparing to work under formal governance regimes.

Upcoming in Volume Two -The Prompt Artist

If the first volume of this trilogy taught structure, the second will teach resonance.
The Prompt Engineer has shown that clarity is a form of control that language, when disciplined, can guide intelligence with precision.
But language can do more than control. It can move.
Where the engineer refines instruction, the artist awakens response.

In The Prompt Artist, we turn from the logic of phrasing to the emotion of expression.
The focus shifts from how to make a model obey to how to make it listen.
This is the territory of tone, rhythm, metaphor, and narrative the invisible forces that give language its depth.
Just as an orchestra responds differently to the same score under different conductors, an AI system can respond differently to the same instruction under different voices.
The artist learns to shape that voice.

This second volume explores prompting as collaboration.
Where the engineer's work ends with coherence, the artist's begins with interpretation.
It will show how prompts can become sketches, moods, or performances invitations rather than directives.
The artist uses syntax the way a painter uses light: not to define the world, but to reveal it.

Readers will learn:

How tone transforms reasoning.

How metaphor, allusion, and symbolism guide model imagination.

How visual and literary styles can be fused in multimodal prompting.

How aesthetic structure — pacing, rhythm, repetition — affects coherence and emotional response.

How to create creative tension between precision and freedom without losing direction.

The book will also explore the philosophy of digital authorship.
When human and artificial voices blend, who becomes the storyteller?
When imagination is shared, what does originality mean?
The Prompt Artist will not only answer these questions it will inhabit them.

Stylistically, Volume Two will feel different.
Where The Prompt Engineer was deliberate and architectural, The Prompt Artist will be fluid and lyrical.
It will read like a masterclass in composition, showing how the same structural discipline can now serve beauty and feeling.
Its examples will include poetry, image generation, music, and dialogue all treated as acts of artistic reasoning.

At its heart, the book will argue that creativity is not the opposite of clarity, but its evolution.
Once the reader understands how intelligence thinks, they are ready to explore how it dreams.
The engineer builds the instrument; the artist learns to play it.

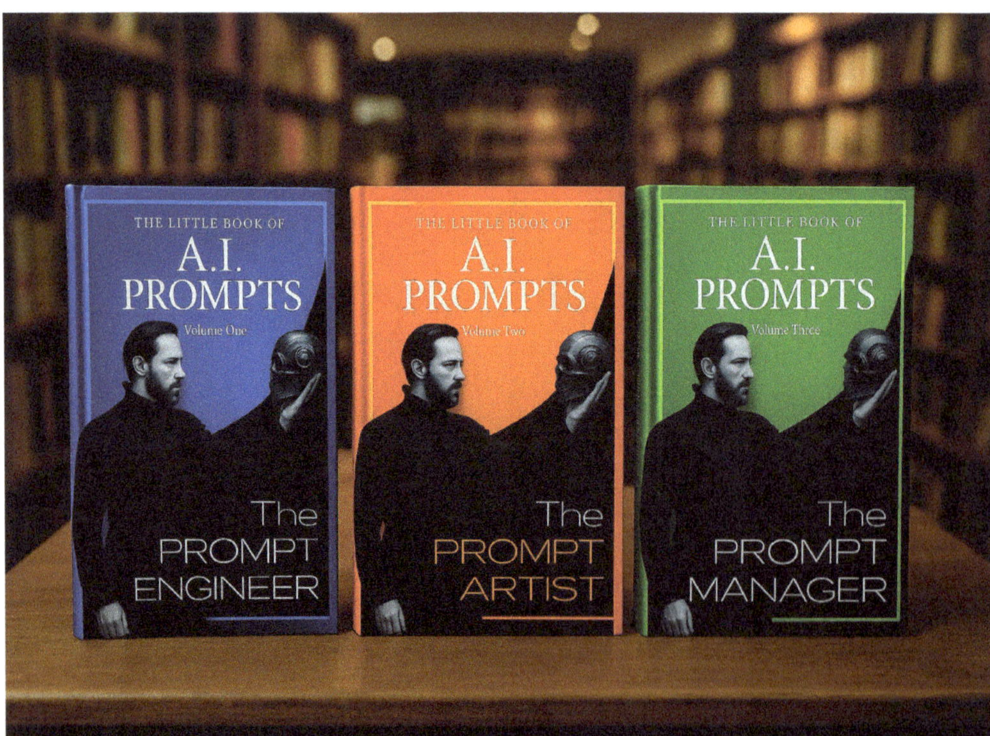

Legal Disclaimer

All examples, scenarios, and frameworks in this book are provided for educational and illustrative purposes only.
No section should be interpreted as legal, medical, or financial advice.
The author and publisher accept no responsibility for any loss or damages arising from use or misuse of the content herein.
Readers are encouraged to apply independent verification and professional judgment in all applications of AI-related material.

www.ingramcontent.com/pod-product-compliance
Lightning Source LLC
LaVergne TN
LVHW060030210926
848481LV00013B/3827

* 9 7 8 1 9 1 9 3 5 1 7 6 6 *